NOTHING BUT $NET

by

Michael W. LeBlanc

Foreward

Don Williams awoke in a cold sweat. He sat up in bed and planted his feet firmly on the floor as he wiped his eyes, trying to get back to reality. He had just been jolted from a nightmare in which he found himself being handcuffed and shoved into the back seat of a patrol car at 6:00 in the morning.

He stumbled into the bath room and splashed cold water on his face. Looking into the mirror he could only see the horror in his eyes. He was replaying the bad dream when he heard a loud banging on his front door. "Who could that be at 6:00 a.m.?" he mumbled as he pulled on his robe.

As he approached the front door, he could see the forms of three people through the door's frosted glass but because they were just out-of-focus shapes through the opaque glass, he could not make out who they were any more than they could identify him. He opened the door to three deputies. One of the deputies ask, "Are you Don Williams?"

With some hesitation he answered, "Yes, is there a problem?"

One of the deputies, waving an arrest warrant under his nose, said, "you're under arrest!" They instructed him to put on some clothes, as he will be going to downtown lockup this morning to be photographed and fingerprinted prior to arraignment.

Don, unable to full comprehend what was happening, could only see the red and blue lights flashing on top of the Patrol Car parked in his driveway! "Shit, what're the neighbors thinking about this?!" he thought.

One of the deputies follows him to his closet, as he proceeded to dress. Don's wife Karen had by this time put on her robe and anxiously asked Don, "What's going on?"

“I don’t know,” he answered. “I don’t know! Call our Attorney.”

As Don is handcuffed and put in the back seat of the car, he looked back to see Karen standing at the front door, crying. She managed to shout through her tears, “I’ll contact our attorney and be at the courthouse as soon as I can get there.”

Moments later, Don, looking into the mirror, realized this was just a horrible dream. He sighed deeply and headed back to bed, thanking God that this was just a bad dream! Karen asks. “Are you ok?”

“Yes,” he said softly. “It was just a bad dream.” He had no way of knowing that this dream could be a harbinger of bad things to come!!

Chapter 1

Don Williams, 50, was living a beautiful life. His wife, Karen and his two sons, Lemmy and Mark had a wholesome upbringing in the small community of Empire City, New York. Don, having grown up in Empire, was a star basketball player at Niagara High School. His proud parents, Dean and Ann Williams are leaders of the community. Dean, a Baptist minister and Ann, a teacher at Niagara High School are the idea couple living modestly in a country home on 2 acres just outside the city limits of Empire City.

Don graduated from Empire State University, the local University. Empire State, with an enrollment of six thousand students, is a member of the Great Lake Conference, a small Division I conference consisting of 8 schools, all located in the Northeast.

Don majored in construction management and played on the basketball team averaging eight points a game. Once out of college, he joined Big Jim's Construction Company, a local company as a small project superintendent.

He and Karen, his High School sweetheart, married when he turned twenty-six. Karen was a kind, beautiful woman, a giving person. A graduate with a degree in psychology, she understood – and accepted – her husband's mood swings and did everything to support him. An only child, she was raised by two doting parents. She was a good wife who loved her husband as much as one could love another.

Karen's parents moved to Buffalo to care for her grandparents. She saw them mostly on holidays. Don and Karen spent most weekends with Don's parents, going to Church, followed by cookouts in the backyard.

Don's singular claim to fame in basketball occurred when in the state high school regional finals, Don made both ends of a one and one free throws to win the game by one point with 2 seconds left on the clock.

That moment would stay with him in life after he was carried off the court in front of the hometown fans and he was featured on the front page of the local newspaper sports section.

Everywhere he went in town, he was cheered, pelted on the back and was just up to at as a home town hero. The euphoria was short-lived when the next week, the basketball team was drummed by upstate Grant High School 63-44 and eliminated from the State Tournament.

Still, Don felt the magic that being a hero brings. He noticed a certain feeling, an air of superiority, when around others. After all, he was well-known in Empire City, a town of some 22,000 people. Even attending Sunday Service at his Dad's Church, The Full Gospel Baptist Church Fellowship, he was something of a distraction from the sermon. Life was just fun and at that moment, he felt so alive.

In their third year of marriage, they announced the coming of their first child, Mark. He was eight pounds and twenty-one inches in length. A beautiful son and the Williamses were so proud as were the grandparents. Then along came Lemmy three years later, similar in size to Mark. The home at that point was a little small so Don added on to the house with another bedroom and bath. He also added a large den with a nice covered patio. The job, the kids, the newly renovated house and a happy wife, life couldn't get any better!

Like all newlyweds with small children, life moved quickly, changing diapers, then pre-school, youth sports, baseball, basketball and soccer Don's job afforded him the opportunity to move upward by starting his own construction company with Big Jim's blessings.

He would concentrate on jobs that Big Jim did not want to take on, which was great for Don's company.

Chapter 2

As the kids grew older, Don became an avid supporter of the high school and the College. He chaired several high school fundraising events and made many new friends through those events.

At the college, he was asked to investigate and analyze the aging of the buildings on campus. This task put him directly in touch with the administration and its construction needs. He learned first-hand that someday the college would need to build or renovate the old basketball arena, a nice job that he hoped to bid on and get.

Don also having played a little golf growing up was encouraged by Karen to join the country club, take lessons, and play on Saturday mornings with a group of men, just to get his mind off his business.

Life has a way of creeping up on one and Mark, his oldest son was suddenly a senior at Empire State. Mark is a smart kid, not real athletic, like Lemmy. Mark is more the engineer type, which thrilled Don. Mark's interest was in becoming a mechanical engineer and he began tinkering with small motors and having them perform tasks that most humans would rather not do.

Lemmy, a freshman, earned a spot on the basketball team at Empire State. On the court, he was quick and a good defensive player. At 6' 2," he concentrated on his shooting, earning All- District honors at Niagara High School, a nice and impressive award. He parlayed his hardwood prowess into a scholarship to Empire State. Don and Karen felt blessed that both their sons were attending Empire State. It was nice to have both sons close to home.

As Don played golf more frequently, he found his game was improving and he joined the Saturday morning golf gang. Roughly sixteen men tee it up every Saturday morning and divide up into competitive groups and play for $5 per point. Don had never gambled in his life on anything but his business.

His Dad, being a Baptist minister, would have been disappointed in him for gambling. Even now, he knew that Don drank occasionally and Don's dad believed the Devil was behind both deficiencies. Therefore, his cautious temperament collides with his religious background. However, Don has always had high self-esteem and super self-confidence! After all, hadn't he won a huge game in front of hundreds when the game was on the line!

Don was also extremely competitive which helped him grind through his golf game on Saturdays. On any given Saturday, one can lose up to forty dollars or win a little more depending on your team members. Anyway, for Don, getting through the nerves on the first few Saturdays was a huge accomplishment that he was proud of. His sixteen-handicap played well from the white tees and after a few weeks, Don had become the popular pick by the captain of the team he would play with on that morning. Don was so pleased when, on the first Saturday, his split of the team's winning was fifty-five dollars. It was a special feeling sliding those crisp bills into his pocket. It seemed almost too easy and he had fun playing competitively.

There were always some interesting and fun men who showed up on those Saturdays. They came from all walks of life: attorneys, a doctor, a lounge owner, an automobile salesman, and so on. They all brought their gigs and their personalities every Saturday, imposing them on each other and the fun would begin. After the round, they all enjoy a cold one and a good sandwich. Life at the Club was certainly an escape for all of them as they traded stories of their week. One could always hear a new joke, which only added to the fun.

After the round, Don generally would swing by the grocery store to pick up the evening's food that he would grill on his new large patio. The food would taste much better when he spent the winnings of the day on the night's meal. Of course, the boys were there with some of their friends if there is not some other function that they would be attending that night. Yes, Don pretty much had it all and his life was fun and comfortable with Karen and his family.

One Monday morning Don got a call at his office from the local school board administrator letting him know he was not the low bidder on the county elementary school addition. The low bid was $1.75 million and Don's company bid $1.85 million, a hundred thousand dollars more.

Don's anticipated profit of 6.5% would equate to a nice $120,000. Don was disappointed and was already planning to spend that money on new equipment, some needed home improvements, and a nice overseas vacation trip for him and Karen.

Chapter 3

That morning, more bad news followed when he learned that the small shopping center he was working on in the city of Empire was running over his bid amount because of increased prices in labor and material.

He immediately got with his comptroller and with all the information at hand at the moment, they figured they would lose approximately $60,000 if they could wrap the job up in next 60 days, or less. Wow, what a bad start to his week. Don was a good businessman and had a nest egg of some $230,000 in his bank account to cover shortfalls as they occurred. His total estimated annual construction goal was seven million dollars.

Targeting a profit of 6%, his projected annual profit after overhead and expenses, was approximately $420,000. That was a comfortable annual income for him and Karen. Don also had a line of credit at the bank of two hundred thousand dollars, a line which he had never drawn on. Construction is a tough business and making a profit through all the pitfalls of the industry is a day-to-day grind.

Don, needing to clear his head, went to lunch at Vinney's Sport Bar that day. Vinney was one of the golfers Don played with on Saturday mornings. They had become good friends through the golf outings and Don's frequent lunches at Vinney's. Vinney, knew the county district attorney and his small bookie operation at the bar was considered off-limits by local law enforcement and never bothered. Vinney would book small bets by college kids on all sports and book his close friends on larger bets.

Don, feeling disappointed that day, sat at the bar and ordered a Martini. Vinney, noticed his sad demeanor and knowing Don had never ordered a martini at lunch, asked what was up with him that day.

"Vinney I've had a bad business morning," don admitted. "I lost a job by a $100 thousand and I'm behind on a job I could lose up to $60,000. So, I just need to cool off and this seems like a good place to do that."

Vinney told Don to just relax. He would take care of his drink and lunch today. Vinney was in a good mood and couldn't hide his latest triumph from Don. Vinney pulled out twenty one-hundred-dollar bills and told Don that the two thousand was the result of his bet on the Chicago Bears football team this past weekend.

Don, being very naïve in that department, asked Vinney how he did that. Vinney said, "Well, Don, my son Timmy is a trainer for the Bears. He attends every practice, wraps ankles, delivers pain pills and just in general is very close to the players and their ills.

"He called me Saturday afternoon before Sunday's game and told me that the starting quarterback for the Bears injured his throwing arm in warm-ups Saturday. He has a heating pad on it but as he was throwing a pass, a lineman had backed up into him and his wrist and arm crashed into the lineman's helmet.

My son said he won't be playing tomorrow. "Normally, the wire service puts out the Injury list of players before the game," Vinny explained, "but I was able to place my bet with my bookie before the news hit Sunday Morning!"

"Tell me more," Don implored.

"Well," Vinney said, "the odds were Green Bay laying 7.5 points. Green Bay was the home team laying the points meant they would have to win by 8 points to cover the spread. Yesterday, the backup quarterback for the Bears threw 2 interceptions, one for a return of a touchdown. The final score was 34-10, Green Bay. Therefore, because I had an inside track on this play, I won."

Don asked Vinney if that was legal what he had done. "Any edge you can get on gambling, you take it!" Vinney replied, a wide grin spread across his ecstatic face. He told Don that he wanted to introduce him to his bookie, Golden, and Don could bet directly with him and get in on some easy money!

"Vinney, I am not sure I want to get hung up in that. I've got a lot on my plate already and another worry is just something I do not need."

Vinney nodded, slung a rag over his shoulder and said, "Don, I'll just let you know what's going on and at that time you can decide. Look, man, this is as close to a lock as you can get! I mean Timmy knows more than any Vegas handicapper."

"Okay, just keep me posted," Don said as he finished off his sandwich and got up to leave.

The next Saturday morning when Don arrived at the Club, he was met by Vinney in the parking lot. That seemed odd to Don, but Vinney couldn't wait to share his thoughts that morning.

"Don, we have got a 'Lock' tomorrow on the Bears game! The total is 39.5 and there is no way San Francisco and the Bears can score that many points."

"Whoa, slow down," said Don, throwing up both hands. "I have no idea what you are talking about!"

"Sorry Don, I forgot you are not into gambling. The 'Total' is the number of points that will be scored in the game by BOTH teams. One can bet either over or under on the total points scored. The play is the under the total of 39.5 points."

"How do you know?" Don asked quizzically.

Vinney smiled at Don, looked around to see if anyone is close by. Vinney couldn't wait to explain his theory. Speaking as if Don had never played sports and knew nothing about playing conditions and injuries, he said, "First thing, Don, is the weather tomorrow. A low pressure is predicted and is going to bring in 3-6 inches of rain for the 3:00 p.m. kick-off, Central time."

"The Bears Stadium, Soldier Field has the worst drainage system in the league. The sod needs to be replaced and every time it rains, the field turns into mud and water puddles near the sidelines. Plus, throwing the ball will be difficult with 15-20 mile-an-hour winds associated with the rain.

"In addition, San Francisco's best running back is hurt and that is the meat of their team. The Bears' strategy is to run the ball since the backup quarterback will start. So, the clock will continue to run because nobody will try passing. When there is an incomplete pass, the clock stops. It won't tomorrow. Running the ball will be the strategy with a very wet field! It's a lock Don!"

Chapter 4

"Now is the time to get down, Don, Now!"

Don was a little thrown off by Vinney's aggressiveness, but it appeared he had some valid points. Don knew about bad weather at football games and a wet ball and a wet field certainly add to the sloppiness of the game, Vinney's assumptions to the contrary notwithstanding. So, Don said, "What do I need to do?"

"Let's go into the Club and use the phone, I'll call Golden." With that, they headed off to the locker room where there was a private room and a private phone for the members.

Vinney called Golden and said I want to introduce you to a new player. His name is Don Williams. He's trustworthy and I back him up one hundred percent." Vinney handed the phone to Don and said to Golden, "Good morning."

Golden replied, in a deep and raspy voice, a voice of someone who had smoked all his life, "Hello Don, look forward to having you on board. Look this is what I will do with you, since you are Vinney's friend. I'll set you up with a $5,000 line of credit. Once I owe you five grand, I pay. I pay on Tuesdays and collect on Mondays, understood? Same for you, once you get to $5000 that you owe me, then, I collect on Mondays. I operate on an all-cash basis. You can just pay Vinney and I'll get the money from him to make it easy on you. Does that work Don?"

"Yes, that will work," Don replied, still uncertain of what he was doing.

Vinney whispers to Don to ask him about the Bears game and the Total. Don, by now thoroughly confused, said to Golden, "I want to bet the over on the Bears game, what is the number?"

Vinney almost crapped in his pants! He grabbed the phone from Don and said to Golden, "You have to admire his honesty, right?" Never does a better tell the bookie what he wants to bet first and then ask for the odds! A dishonest bookie will slant the line in favor of the bookie and not the person betting. For the bookie, it's like seeing the other person's card in a poker game before the bet.

On the other end, Golden asks Vinney, "Where did you get this guy?" Don, embarrassed at his gullibility, could hear Golden laughing his butt off. Golden tells Vinney, "Let me talk to him, I'll be straight with him."

Golden says to Don, "Don it is unfortunate and I am being straight with you, the total on the game is 38.5 as of this morning. Vegas is aware that the weather will be a factor, so they have lowered the number from 39.5 to 38.5."

"Golden can you hold for a moment?" Don asked as he covered the phone with his hand and told Vinney that the total was now 38.5.

Vinney pauses for a second and winks at Don and whispers, "we're still good!'

"I want to place a bet on the over for the Bears game at 38.5 points," Don said, returning to Golden.

"Great how much do you want to bet?"

"Five hundred."

"Sorry, I don't take any anything less than a thousand. (To win $1,000, the bettor has to lay the juice or 10% to win a $1,000). Don, feeling even more embarrassed from his first mistake, swallows hard and practically whispered, "Okay."

11. Golden, as always, a professional, always repeats the bet back to the bettor to make sure they are on the same page. "You have $1,100 on the Over 38.5 total points on the Bears, Frisco game tomorrow to win a $1,000. Don looks at Vinney and repeats out loud the bet for his friend's benefit, "I have a $1,100 bet on the over 38.5 total points on the Bears/Frisco game tomorrow. Vinney screams, "No, you want the under, the under, the *UNDER* on the Total!"

"You must think I am an idiot," Don said to Golden. "Please excuse me, I'm a little nervous. I want the under on the total, not the over please."

"Cancel the over the total on the Bears game of 38.5 points to betting the under the total on the Bears game of 38.5 points," Goden said, his voice flat and even, as if he did this every day – which he did. "Is that correct Don Williams?"

"Yes, sir, and thank you for your patience with me". Golden told Don to get his number from Vinney, so in the future he can call Golden direct. Don thanked him and hung up.

Don turned and looked at Vinney. His face was beet red and he felt like he had been man-handled by a couple of wrestlers. He wondered, *what have I done? I've got a $1,100 bet on a football game! Wow, I must look like an easy target.* As they walked out the men's locker room, Vinney slapped Don on the back and said," Don, you're going to love watching this game, the sweat is so real and the euphoria you will get from placing the bet, is exhilarating, but the real rush is when you know your bet was right!"

As they walked into the bar area, Don could not resist ordering a bloody mary, double vodka. His nerves are shot and his morning as turned into a blur. It showed in his golf game that morning as he didn't break a 100, lost sixty-two dollars, and headed home immediately after the round to find some comfort in his world.

Chapter 5

"LUCY, YOU GOT SOME 'SPLAINING TO DO!"

On his way home, it occurred to Don that he could not tell anyone what he had done, certainly not Karen. He found himself getting starting to get really pissed off at Vinney for the way he approached him in the parking lot and then pushed so hard to connect him with Golden.

In a way, Don felt dirty, betting a $1,100 with a bookie, someone he didn't even know personally. Don did get Golden's number from Vinney, so he could back out of the bet if need be. For now, though, he decided to shower, take a quick nap and try to forget the morning's events.

When he arrived home, he found Karen in the kitchen preparing a chicken dish for the night. The boys would be coming home later to watch a college football game and to share in some refreshments. He felt even guiltier when he saw his wife in the kitchen, oblivious to what he'd done.

She just wants to be a good wife and a loving mother, he thought as he watched her go about preparing dinner. After all, she and Don had worked hard to get ahead in life and their lifestyles were comfortable and peaceful.

As Don replayed the fiasco of earlier that day, his competitive juices started to kick in. After all, he did have a$1,100 to lose and he didn't have to pay unless he loses $5,000. Misgivings aside, he secretly wanted to win that bet, just to prove he was not totally crazy. *Give it to Vinney, he does have some good reasons why the game will be low scoring*. Don kissed Karen and excused himself to lie down in the bedroom. He promised to share a glass of wine with her around 5:00 that afternoon, before the boys arrived.

He took an unusually long, hot shower in an attempt to wash off the physical and emotional strain and the moral stain he had experienced earlier in the day. Afterward, he dressed and sank into his bed. He was home, in his comfort zone, and feeling more secure. He used the break in the day to attempt to reintroduce himself to who he really was and to get back to being Don Williams.

He awoke about an hour later and strolled into the living room, trying to convey the image that everything was normal. The boys were already there, laughing and joking with each other. "How was your golf game?" Lemmy asked.

"Not good today" Don replied. "Couldn't get off the tee, hit a lot of traps, just a long, hot day."

"I saw Vinny this afternoon and he said the same thing about your golf game today," Mark said. Don being curious asked " Where did you see him?"

"At his sports bar" Mark replied. "I bet ten dollars with him on the Nebraska game tonight against Iowa State."

Don quietly seethed at Vinney and asked, "Who did you bet on?" *Now Vinney is corrupting my son.*

"I bet Nebraska giving 18.5 points."

Don, very curious asks Mark, "why that bet?"

Mark grinned broadly because he wanted to let his dad know that he knew something about sports and besides, he has a part-time job at Verizon and makes $12 an hour or roughly $120 a week. It was his money he was putting at risk. "Well, Nebraska always wins at home and they are a great running team. Iowa State is a passing team and guess what? The weather for the kickoff is calling for torrential rains and 20-25 mile-an-hour wind. Not good for a passing team!"

Don's memory came around in full force! This is the same shit he heard from Vinney this morning about the weather affecting the game. Don, wanting to seem interested in Mark's bet and wanting him to know he knew a little bit about wagering, asked, "Do you know the *total* on the game?"

Mark replied, "Yes sir, its seventy-two points!" Don, incredulous, almost shouted says, "Seventy-two points? If the weather's that bad, how in the heck are they going to score that many points?"

"I don't know, Dad, but I can tell you that these Vegas guys are pretty accurate on a lot of odds and if they put the number at seventy-two, you can bet it will be close to that number!"

I've got to see this game and how each team handles the ball in all that weather, Don thought to himself. It'll give me a preview into what the Bears game will look like tomorrow.

He picked up the TV remote and found The Weather Channel. He wanted to see if the same weather pattern would hit Chicago on Sunday. The Weather Channel always does a weather in motion and puts a timeline on the movement of systems moving from one area to the other. His concerns were extinguished when he saw that same low-pressure system that would hit Lincoln, Nebraska later that afternoon and night would hit Chicago the following day, as well.

Staring at The Weather Channel, he found himself caught up in an out-of-body experience. To make matters worse, there was a mirror hanging over the fireplace mantle and he caught himself looking at his reflection. *Look at me, caught up now in all kinds of things and worries that I never thought would bring me to this moment. Don, you are a sad sack.*

Chapter 6

"Guys, Dinner is served," Karen called from the kitchen. The meal consisted of baked chicken, roasted potatoes and a green salad, all the things she did best.

The game was scheduled to begin in about half an hour, but no one mentions it because meal time was almost a sacred ritual for the Williams family. Everyone was healthy and doing well and savored their time together. Karen poured Don a glass of white wine. It was good to take the hearty laughter of the boys and to listen to their week's experiences. He hoped the combination of everyone's being together and the wine would settle his nerves.

Lemmy's basketball workouts were going well and he revealed to the family that he could start as a freshman. Mark said that there would be a job seminar coming to the college around Christmas break. It would feature companies interviewing for graduates that qualified for jobs at their firms.

Don inquired of Mark what his initial thoughts were on what he would like to do. He said he was interested in working for a firm that invented things like drone development and artificial intelligence with robots, etc. "I just love that kind of stuff," he said. "Also, I have a customer that owns a garage and he has invited me to visit him and see how he repairs engines and everything else he does in his garage. I'm excited to look under the hood, so to speak. It should be fun!"

As dinner wound down, Karen began to clear the table. Don and the boys took their plates to the Kitchen where Don rinsed the plates and silverware and put them in the dishwasher. The boys thanked their mother for the meal and retired to the family room to watch the game. A few minutes later, Don joined them and took his seat in his recliner, the best seat in the house.

He was curious to hear and see the pre-game commentary. He noticed the driving sheets of rain in the background as the two announcers described the obviously terrible playing conditions and speculated as to what each team would have to concentrate on to be competitive.

As the team captains met in the center of the field for the coin toss, the TV cameras panned the stadium so that the viewing audience could see the preparations each fan had made for the wet and windy conditions. Parkas, rain suits, hoodies, hats and programs draped over their heads. Anything and everything was being done to protect them from this storm.

Nebraska won the toss and elected to receive. The kickoff by Iowa State was horrible; the ball sailed only about ten feet off the ground and hit on Nebraska's 30 yard line. The up back fielded the ball and returned it to the 'Huskers' 40-yard-line. The cameras could barely pick up the players who were all but obscured by the downpour.

Don thought it might be fun to watch what more closely resembled a swimming pool party than a football game. The first play from scrimmage, the Nebraska tailback plowed off right tackle where he was hit by Iowa State's linebacker. The ball carrier broke the tackle because there was too much slipping and sliding for a solid hit or to get a solid grip. The tailback broke to the outside and outran the secondary for a 60-yard touchdown. Mark is ecstatic. Seven-zip Nebraska! Mark has cut the 18.5 margin of victory down to 11.5 in the first few seconds of the first quarter.

Don's face turned red from a combination of dread, frustration and outright anger. He had just witnessed a defense that could not get good footing and the offense definitely had the advantage. As the game progressed, it became obvious that Mark had made a good bet.

It was Nebraska leading, thirty-four to seven at halftime. Nebraska had covered the spread in just the first half, not to mention the Total looks so favorable for the over the seventy-two points. Don suddenly had serious concerns for the Bears game total for the day. He slipped off to his office and closed the door. Calling Vinney at his Sports Bar, he spat, "Vinney, are you watching the Nebraska game?"

"No why?"

"This storm has not done a damned thing to slow the scoring down. Nebraska is going to score 80 points by itself! Vinney, we've made a bad bet, I'm so upset…"

"Hold on, Don," Vinney interrupted. "You can't compare apples to oranges. That's a college game. The field is different from the Bears' field. Artificial turf vs. grass. College games score more than the pros. We have a solid bet, don't bail on me! It's natural to have the first bet jitters. Relax, my friend, and have trust in the information, trust the Vegas line, and trust that these games are two completely different situations. We'll be victorious.

"Don, go to bed early, think about something else."

Don said, "I hope to hell you're right. I'm just not feeling good about any of this."

By 8:30 p.m. Don was washed out. He told the boys good night and told Karen he was retiring to the bedroom. He told himself he'd put football out of his mind and to also try to forget about tomorrow's reckless bet. Karen understood he had had a long day and told him she would join him shortly. By the time she got to the bedroom, Don was sound asleep. Of course, taking two sleeping pills instead of one, will do it every time.

Chapter 7

Don awoke around 7:30 a.m. He did his normal bathroom routine and headed to the kitchen where Karen had already made coffee. She asked him how he slept. “Surprisingly well,” he replied.

“Would you like some eggs and bacon?” she asked.

“That would be great sweetheart. I apologize for the lack of energy yesterday. I know I just wasn’t myself.”

She responded with a big hug as she said, “I know you have got a lot on your mind and that’s okay. Today will be a wonderful day and you will feel a like yourself again”

Karen saying the words that it will be a wonderful day just brought home the reality of the huge bet he had placed on that day’s game. Under his breath, he cursed himself, saying he just didn’t want to have it hanging over his head. *I do not want to live like this!*

After breakfast, Don and Karen headed out to the 10:30 a.m. church service where his father was to give his Sunday sermon. The boys, having gone to the Wednesday night Service decided to sleep in so, it would be just Don and Karen attending the Dean Williams sermon.

As was the custom, his parents stood at the church entrance to welcome everyone parishioners. It was a wonderful tradition, especially for the guests to meet Dean and Ann for the first time. Don and Karen got their usual hugs from his parents and took their seats, third row from the alter on the left side of the church. The attendance was shaping up to be a good turnout. Don admired his father for his untiring effort to deliver a heartfelt and meaningful message to the congregation. Pastor Dean felt a deep appreciation and a great challenge to deliver the word that would hit home and perhaps change somebody's life that day. After all, God's work is never done and it's very special to hear the word of the Lord from an articulate Preacher.

At the beginning of each service, *Amazing Grace* was sung by the Choir and congregation as church deacons entered the church, parading down the enter aisle. The cross, held by one of the deacons, led the way with the Bible held high in the air by a second deacon as Rev. Dean followed the procession to the altar.

It was a moving event and set the tone for a spiritual day. The parishioners of The Full Gospel Baptist Church Fellowship respected the Sunday Service and contrary to a growing trend of casual dress, all wore their Sunday best. Pastor Dean wore a royal blue suit with a white shirt and glowing gold tie. The atmosphere in the Church was one of devout reverence and deep spiritual belief in the Lord.

Upon arriving at the Altar, the minister, as always, opened with a prayer. The choir, singing low but effectively, created somber setting for the congregation, leaving no doubt that this was a house of worship. Everyone, members and visitors alike, were welcomed to the service. He asked that guests to please complete the guest card in the front pockets of the pews. He had such a warm voice and a great smile, it gave everyone a good feeling of being there this Sunday.

Don, looking up at his father with a since of pride, was aware that his parents had given him so many great lessons in his life that had provided him with a rich and happy life. At the same time, he couldn't shake the lurking dark thought that lingered in Don's mind, refusing to go away even as his father started his sermon. Oh yes, that nagging bet, the thought of gambling $1,100 on a football game gnawed at his conscience.

His father began with a reading from Samuel 30:6: *David found strength in the Lord his God.*

Then raising his voice, the minister said, "you must confront your Weakness." *Oh God, he's is talking about me! How does he know what I am going through*? Don prayed silently, *Dear Lord, please get me through this service and this day!*

His father, hammered home his message from the pulpit raising his voice to a pitch as he did so. "Regardless of what problems you face or how inadequate you might feel in any given situation, be it in the business world, on the home front, on the sports field, or even in your family life, you must surrender it in prayer to God. Ask him to give you strength to handle any situation you find yourself in. Once you accept this and believe He can and will do it, you can move forward with confidence in the knowledge that God's grace is sufficient to enable you to overcome your weakness."

Don, kicking himself mentally, thought, *Why Don didn't you have more strength to stand up to Vinney yesterday morning and say "Vinney, I can't do this, period*?"

Pastor Dean was adept at pulling the heart strings of the congregation as he asked if they could overcome their insecurities. "The only way to a strong and successful life is let God in it," he implored. "Then, your day will be filled with peace and joy. "Your spirit will lift you and you in turn, will lift others.

At the end of every service, Pastor Dean stood at the foot of the altar, led the congregation in prayer, and invited whoever wanted to come to the front of the church, with everyone in the church as witnesses, and get a personal prayer and blessing from Pastor Dean and commit to join the church by accepting Jesus Christ as their savior.

On this Sunday, as if the hand of God had been laid upon their shoulders, a young couple came forward, followed by an older couple, and then, an elderly woman and her daughter. In all, six souls filled with the spirit, walked down to receive Pastor Dean's blessing.

The choir, singing softly, provided the perfect pull atmosphere for accepting Jesus. Pastor Dean beamed in the glow of a productive Sunday, feeling that it was truly a great day for the church. When the service had ended, Pastor Dean and his deacons walked to the back of the Church where they greeted all of the parishioners as they departed.

It had already been scheduled that Don and Karen would meet his mom and dad at Deano's Steak House and sit at their reserved table in the back of the restaurant. Don suffered an anxiety attack as the words of his father' sermon hit him hard and remained with him throughout the meal. He had trouble staying within the speed limit on the way to the Restaurant.

Chapter 8

Don dropped Karen off at the front door while he parked the car. She was seated at their table by Andy, the host. Don had to use the restroom and luckily, the bar was on the way to the restroom but conveniently tucked in the back of the restaurant so that no one can see who is in the bar.

Don, feeling insecure and nervous, stopped and asked Billy, the bartender, to pour him a straight shot of Scotch. He downed it quickly and then says, "One more." He drank that one in the same manner and then hit the restroom. As he headed to his table, he saw that his parents were already moving through the restaurant shaking hands, smiling and enjoying their status as the leaders of the community.

As they all sat at the table, Don and Karen tell Dean that it was a inspirational sermon and an overall wonderful service. Dean, feeling especially good about his sermon, surprised everyone at the table by announcing that he is going to order a cocktail and, partially in jest, asked out loud for God to forgive him. Merlene, the waitress doesn't hesitate and says yes sir Mr. Dean. The girls, feeling uninhibited now, follow suit and ordered a glass of white wine each. Don decided to go for it and ordered an Old Fashion. Dean commented that that sounded good.

Somewhere it is written that Baptists do not drink or gamble. But maybe today the good Lord will give a pass and besides every once and while it is okay to celebrate a wonderful day with family. The meal was delicious and Dean and Don both have another cocktail. What those at the table did not know was that Don was duplicating his routine on two more occasions when he went to the restroom. Don also checked out the NFL broadcast where they are previewing all of the games and he notices that at Soldier Field, it is pouring down buckets of rain! *Just what the doctor ordered* he thought to himself as the hiccups took over his speech.

Lunch ended around 2:00 p.m. Game time was 3:00 p.m. Don and Karen hugged his parents and told them goodbye. Don handed the keys to Karen and asked her to drive because he was aware that he'd had too much to drink to risk driving home.

Don was slightly blitzed and said little to Karen in response to her small talk about the service and lunch. She was happy for her father-in-law and for his good day. When they arrive home, Don asked Karen to make coffee while he changed into something more comfortable.

Smiling, she said, "You do whatever you want this afternoon. I have a book I've been meaning to read and with the boys gone this afternoon the house will be quiet."

He retreated to the bedroom and changed clothes and prepared to watch the game. Back in the kitchen, he poured a cup of coffee and Karen went to the bedroom to change. He slid the liquor cabinet open and poured Benedictine and brandy into his coffee just to top off the taste of the liquor he has been drinking all day. B&B sweetened the coffee. It also offered a powerful addition to anyone's day of drinking!

It was fifteen minutes before kickoff and Don had the TV on the Bears game. It was still raining and people in the stands were sporting parkas, raincoats, hats – just anything to protect from the twenty-mile-an-hour winds and the pounding rain. Sitting in his easy chair, he could barely see the TV. His eyes are half shut and he could barely talk. The room is spinning and the only way out of this is to go take a nap and plead a little drunk.

Getting up, he said, "Shit on it!" He stumbled to his office, closed the door and called Golden's number, thinking to himself, *I can't handle this, I am going to cancel the bet.* As he tried to dial the number, his fingers wouldn't cooperate. He tried again and was rewarded with an annoying busy signal. He kept dialing until finally, after six tries, the phone rang. Golden barked into the phone and Don, in a stupor, slurred, "Golden, Don Williams here."

"Hey, Don, what can I do for you?"

"Golden, I want to cancel my bet on the Bears!"

"Sorry, Don, they just kicked off and I don't cancel or take bets once the game has started. And besides Don, Frisco just returned the kickoff to the Bears' fifteen yard line."

Don's heart sank. He was suddenly living his worst nightmare. Nobody can tackle in a driving rain. Don, almost in surrender mode said, "Okay, thanks, Golden and good luck." He hung up and under his breath, said to himself, "Why I am wishing that S.O.B. good luck? He's stealing my money!" It was like the time that he thanked a cop for giving him a speeding ticket.

He stumbled back to the TV and noticed that the Forty-Niners kicked a field goal with just a minute and 30 seconds gone on the clock. 3-0 49ers. He sat back in the chair and watched as the Bears lined up to punt from their own 22-yard-line. Then, another fricking nightmare, the snap sailed over the punters head and rolled into the end zone. There was a mad scramble by both teams to cover the ball. The refs, sloshing around in the pooled water, attempted to get to the bottom of the pile. The TV cannot pick up the details among the tangle of bodies obscured by the sheets of rain. The only image that can be made out for certain was the unfocused shot of the refs trying to get to the bottom of the pile.

Finally, they signal safety. The Bears have recovered the ball in their own end zone and that's two points for the 49ers. Five-zip with less than three minutes gone in the game. At this rate the Total will be well over 38.5 by halftime.

Chapter 9

Unable to stand the suspense any longer, he gave up any hope of winning the bet and headed to his bed, telling Karen he just needed some sleep. Falling into bed, he was out almost instantly, snoring his ass off. Karan, realizing he wasn't acting his usual self, wondered what was going on. Even though he was not acting normal, she didn't question him.

Around 7:00 p.m., she awakened him. Still groggy, he was jogged alert when she said that Vinney has called and asked that he call him when he got up. Don immediately thought that the call could only mean that he was out $1,100 and perhaps that Vinney was calling to apologize for convincing him to make that bet. He went to the kitchen, grabbed a glass of water.

He could tell by the kitchen aroma that Karen had cooked fish with roasted potatoes. *Wow, what a woman!* She walked over to him, put her arms around him and asked, "Don, you okay" What's going on?"

"I'm working through some things at work, it's going to be okay. I'll tell you about it tomorrow night, if you do not mind?"

Then he told Karen he would return Vinney's call; it's probably about their golf game next weekend. As Don was dialing Vinney's number, he dreaded hearing the words, *I am sorry Don, I got it wrong*. Too exhausted to fight with Vinney, he said to himself, *I should just wait to talk to him about the game tomorrow*.

Don went ahead and called Vinney at the Sports Bar, however. Ted, the Bartender, answered the phone and Don asked Ted for Vinney. "Can I tell him who is calling?

"Yes, tell him it's Don Williams!

He heard Ted yell, "Hey Vinney it's Don Williams for you." He could hear all the background chatter and the juke box blaring away.

Then Vinney picked up the phone and said "Don, hold on, I'm going to my office for privacy." Shit Don thought, *Yep, we lost and he wants to apologize in private so no one hears him*. Don was put on hold and it seemed like eternity before Vinney picked up the phone and yells to Don, "You are one lucky son of a bitch!"

"What are you saying?" Don implored.

Vinney almost shouting, sang out, "Final 30 to 8 Bears win!"

Don trying to get his head around the Total thought *Under 38 ½, total 38 points*, "Vinney we win?"

"Yes, Vinney. Amen brother, you didn't watch the game?"

"No, I got drunk and couldn't stand the first 3 minutes, looked like a track meet. So, Vinney, why am I lucky?"

"Well Don if you watched the game, you would have seen the Bears with the ball on the 49ers, five-yard line with 40 seconds left and they fucking kneeled down on the final two plays. Game over! That's how you win baby, that's how you win."

"Come by for lunch tomorrow, I got your grand. Golden's runner is changing his route. Golden wants you to enjoy your victory. He says you wanted to cancel the bet and he wished you would have called earlier, Don you are not only lucky but you can't be a chicken shit in this arena. I told you, stick with Pappa Vinney!"

Don plopped down in his chair as he hung up the phone. Looking to the sky he said, "Thank you Jesus, oh God thank you" as he puts both hands together in prayer. He sat there for a minute just breathing hard, trying to control his emotions. As he did so, he felt a tremendous pressure leave his body. Then, he opened his eyes, looked around at his surroundings, saying to himself, "I won, I won, I won!" He stood up, pounded his chest, and thrusting his shoulders back, wanted to yell, "I was right, I am a winner, fucking A!"

He had to hide his excitement as he entered the Kitchen as saw Karen cleaning up. He walks over to her and grabbed her up in a lingering hug. "You are beautiful, I love you so much."

"I am glad you are feeling better," she said, kissing him on the cheek.

Chapter 10

MONDAY, MONDAY

Monday morning Don awoke with a clear head. He jumped out of bed, dressed quickly, grabbed a cup of coffee and headed to the office. He arrives around 8:30 to find Matte, his secretary, already there. "Good morning sunshine, he chirped." She returned the greeting, adding that he had a 10:00 a.m. meeting with Dr. Roy Stevenson at the college. Don says, "Thank you. Matte, I've been so busy I'd forgotten."

It was an important meeting as he'd been awaiting confirmation that he could be awarded the renovation contract for the Empire University gym. fortunately, he was wearing one of his best suits, his shoes were freshly shined, and he sported a bright red tie. He left for the meeting knowing he looked good. He was feeling fantastic in anticipation of the meeting.

He arrived at Stevenson's office fifteen minutes early. He and the University President' friendship went back to their days as students at Empire together. They'd played basketball together, though Don played a lot more minutes than Roy. Being a teammate with someone forms a lifelong bond. They'd remained close throughout the years with both finding success in their respective fields.

The president's receptionist told Don to go on in. "Dr. Stevenson is ready for you." As he started for the door to Stevenson's office, she asked him how he liked his coffee. He took that as a good omen.

"I like one sugar and one cream and thank you." He entered Stevenson's office through a pair of ten-foot-high, stained oak double doors into an office that was huge and tastefully appointed. The office on the fifth floor of the Administration Building was the showcase of university offices – as one might expect. When one walks into this fourteen-foot-high ceiling office, its wood-paneled walls, with floor to ceiling windows overlooking the University, it is unmistakably obvious to the visitor that it's the office of someone really important.

The two old friends meet as Don entered the office. They shook hands and exchanged warm hugs, gives him before they were seated at a small table overlooking the campus. Don, feeling confident and looking good and relaxed, knew that his mind and soul were in a perfect spot to have this meeting with Roy.

The receptionist served the coffee as Roy asked, "Don how are you doing?"

“Well Roy, I’m giving them hell every day.” Then chuckling, he added, “You know, you win some, lose some.” Simultaneously, he thought, *Yessir, I kicked their ass yesterday feeling all proud!*

“So, Don, I want to make your day, so I’ll come right to the point. The board of trustees voted late Friday to award you the new renovation contract for the gymnasium. Congratulations!

“Well thank you so much Roy, but how do I get a contract without a public bid?”

“Don, we just had some construction bonds paid off and we are going back to the market to raise $20 million for this project. Since we bond our student’s tuition, individual donations and our Athletic Foundation funds, we are not using public money to build this project. In other words, we are a private corporation and we can just negotiate the contract with you, as voted”

“In fact,” he continued, we hired an architect about two months ago to come up with a program to determine the scope and magnitude of the job. His name is Bill King, of King and Associates out of Buffalo. His firm has been involved with either designing new college gymnasiums or renovating them. He is quite competent and we need you to meet with him in about two weeks when he returns to do some more onsite work.

“He will have completed his design development phase of the project and will present it to the board. We need your input on pricing, availability of materials, market conditions, etc. You and Bill can huddle at your office and then when you are ready with your cost estimate we will all meet again.”

“What is your time line for construction?” Don asked.

“it’s a rather aggressive one Don, this being October, we would like to begin the first week in March of next year. Bill tells us his architectural plans will be complete around the first of the year and that will give you approximately sixty days to complete the pricing and then mobilize. We need the renovation done in ten months so we can continue to play basketball. The intent is to not miss a game in the gymnasium, so your priority is to get the inside work done first and then we can fence off areas where the outside work is to be done."

Don, exuding the confidence required of the occasion, said, "Roy, I can make it happen"

Roy nodded in agreement and said, "That's why we hired you. Thank you, Don, and I'll be in touch."

"Thank you Roy, We've been friends for a lot of years since we played ball here. I will not let Empire down"!

Don walked out of the elevator on the first floor of the Administration Building gliding on air. He got into his car and headed straight to Vinney's Sports Bar. *Wow, I've gone from the outhouse last Saturday to the White House today.* Of course, he is referring to his spiritual self and the miles in between almost wanting to die vs now when he felt he couldn't get enough of life. *Thank you, Jesus, thank you!*

Chapter 11

Vinney had a huge smile on his face as he greeted Don warmly and hugged him. "Winner, winner, chicken dinner!" Don ordered a beer. The hard stuff would have to wait for tonight when he would break the news to Karen about the new job. He sat at a high-top table and ordered a patty melt and fries. Vinney sidled up, pulling out a small white envelope as he did so, and handed it to Don. Inside, Don found ten crisp, one-hundred-dollar bills.

"I thought Golden paid on Tuesdays and only when either one of us owed $5,000," Don said, puzzled.

"Don, somebody above Golden likes you. In fact, Golden wants you to call him this afternoon about going to Atlantic City to meet his boss. He says they may need you to do some construction work for them."

Taking a first big gulp of draft beer, Don wiped his mouth and said enthusiastically, "Hell yes, I'm on a roll, Vinney!" He asked Vinney to tell him how he knew Golden.

"Well, long story. I was attending a Restaurant Convention in Las Vegas about twenty-five years ago. As I was leaving the airport, I was asked by this short, ball headed man if I wanted a Limo ride to my hotel. He told me cabs were forty-five bucks and he would charge fifty dollars to my hotel. Seemed like a good deal, especially in a Limo, so I said sure. We had a nice conversation on the way to the Hotel. When I told him that I was from Empire, New York, he knew exactly where I was from because he was from Newark, New Jersey. He said he was a bookie there before the local D.A. came down on him. He said driving the Limo was a part time job and dealing blackjack at the Flamingo Casino was his other job.

Golden said he lost his wife in a car accident and had a little girl without a mother. He thought it was important that she have a sound upbringing, so he put her up for adoption. A nice mature couple from upstate New York adopted her and he said he has been in touch with her only on occasion. She graduated from Columbia with a law degree and now has been working for a savings and loan in Manhattan and doing very well. He said he would will see her at Christmas and he said he may have a job for me in few years.

He gave me his number and I have been knowing him ever since he moved back to Newark and is booking again, this time with a legal booking license. His daughter was instrumental in helping him in acquiring the license. That's all I know except that he is a straight shooter and someone you can count on.

That Monday afternoon, Don called Golden and thanked him for the money. "Golden," he said, "I thought we were only going to settle debts on $5,000!"

"Don, I wanted you to get a taste of victory. In this business, fast pay makes long-standing friends, I had a runner collecting in the area, so it was easy to drop off your winnings."

Golden then informed Don that his bosses want to meet him because they have a need for some construction projects in the New Jersey area that they would like to meet a good contractor.

"What type of construction, Golden?"

"I really don't know but they have been building apartments, office buildings and storage units in the past and, Don, my bosses have a lot of money, it will be worth your time. Can you come to Atlantic City a week from tomorrow, Tuesday, the 12th? They will send the jet to pick you up in Empire City and you will stay two nights at their casino hotel and then return on Thursday. The dress is casual and they have their top suite ready for you!"

"Give me a couple of hours to confirm, I may have to move a few things around, but that sounds very enticing."

"Thanks, Don, I'll wait to hear from you."

The proposition piqued Don's interest. *Wow, this could be interesting. I do have a license in Jersey and it's only a three-hour drive to Atlantic City and just two-hours to Newark. This could be doable.* He paid his tab and headed straight to his office to check his calendar for the following week.

When he arrived at his office, Matte told him that Dr. Stevenson wanted to see him the following Monday at his office at 10:00 a.m.

He checked his schedule for the following week and found he was clear to go. He called Golden to confirm the date and the bookie promised to call back with the travel details.

When Don arrived home for the evening, he grabbed a shot of Scotch and poured a glass of wine for Karen as they retreated to the patio to discuss his new venture. He had to be careful in how he would couch the narrative because there could be no mention of gambling and or how he got the invitation – unless the invitation came from someone she knew.

He simply planned to say that Vinney, through his contacts, had friends in the casino business in Atlantic City who want to expand their business and need a reputable contractor to interview.

Karen was familiar with Vinney and his wife Beth and agreed with Don that it was exciting news. Feeling somewhat relieved, Don downed the scotch and walked back to the kitchen to get a refill.

They settled down for a peaceful night with the boys and enjoyed a delicious spaghetti dinner. Don, excited at the prospects of landing two big projects, had trouble falling asleep that night. His mind raced with thoughts about what could become of his newfound prospects! He could not suppress a grin lying there in the darkness. With the new gym renovation coming and the prospect of these new projects in New Jersey, Don could finally envision himself as major contractor, no longer dependent upon picking up projects no one else wanted. *No more nickel and dime work for me*.

The next morning Don received a call from Golden who laid out the details of the trip. The company jet, he said, would pick Don up at the fixed-base operator at the local private airport in Empire City at 10:00 a.m. on Tuesday the 12th.

Empire City boasted an airport that was strictly for private planes – no commercial flights. The airport, operated by an outfit called Chesters, had half-a-dozen hangers that housed roughly ten small planes each. The runway was six thousand feet long, which easily handled accommodated jets, although, not many jets flew in and out of Empire City, except for visiting teams for special sporting events or by other big hitters coming to town.

Chapter 12

Next week could not come fast enough for Don, who was sure his net worth would increase precipitously with the possibility of new construction in the future. He checked with his Construction Insurance Bonding Agent as the University work would certainly require it and perhaps the private work, as well. He had a Bonding capacity of $20 million and he was already planning to seek at least $40 million to cover the increased work load. He anticipated no problems because of his sterling resume and reputation as a builder who delivered on time and on budget.

On Monday morning, the day before he was scheduled to leave for Atlantic City, he attended the 10:00 a.m. meeting at Dr. Stevenson's office. Roy, as Don called his old friend, forgoing the formal "Dr. Robinson," title, informed Don that the Conference was in the process of unifying certain requirements to make the league better. One of the upgrades to be done at the basketball gyms required each gym to install basketball goals that are synchronized with the shot clock. Meaning that when the game clock or the shot clock has run out, the perimeter of the goal backboards would light up in red colors to indicate time had expired. It eliminated any human decision on whether the player has launched the ball toward the goal before the clock ran out or before a half had ended. Replays would still be used, of course, if any last-second shot was contested.

Dr. Stevenson informed Don that he would like to have the goals installed within three weeks to comply with the conference requests. Don assured him that the deadline was reasonable provided the manufactures had them in stock, which they should. He researched the goals and found those most commonly used in college and pro arenas. They ran between $10,000 and $15,000 each, including assembly.

He contacted a company out of Michigan and they assured him they could deliver in two weeks. They emailed him an invoice, which he forwarded to Dr. Stevenson who approved the purchase. Don was given a time and date the goals would arrive. In researching the specs, Don realized he would have to provide an outlet to connect the electrical service to the clock lights built into the fiberglass backboard.

That night, Don packed and got a good night sleep, ready for new opportunities. The following morning, he arrived at Chester's FBO and enters from the parking lot. To his surprise, there are two uniformed pilots are already sitting in the waiting area.

The two pilots stand up and introduced themselves to Don. "I'm Ben," said one and the second simply said "Jerry" as they shook Don's hand. "Nice to meet you," Don responded. Then they asked if he is ready to go as they grabbed his bag while Don made a quick visit to the rest room. Upon leaving the lobby to walk out to the plane, he was taken aback at the size of this beautiful white jet! He learned that it was a Gulfstream 650, one of the most popular corporate jets.

He was greeted at the bottom of the stairs of the plane by a young, red-headed attendant named Cindy. She was dressed in a blue skirt with a white long sleeve shirt and a cute little attendant's hat was perched on her head. She led him up the stairs and once inside, Don was awestruck at the size of the cabin. He was actually able to walk down the aisle of the cabin without having to stoop. *This is certainly first class.* The interior featured white leather chairs and tan carpet on the floor and walls. There were ten huge captain chairs adorned in leather and tan trim on the arm rests.

Cindy directed him to a middle row, window seat. He noticed that there was a TV screen on the back of the seat in front of him. Looking around as discreetly as he could so as not to appear unfamiliar with such trappings, he saw that there was even a restroom in the rear of the plane.

Feeling a bit overwhelmed, he thought, *these boys have a lot of play money*. One of the pilots came back to visit Don as he was getting comfortable. He told to Don that the flight was a short 50 minutes to Atlantic City. He turned on the TV for Don and explained that he could track the trip by using the GPS channel – just like on big commercial planes. "Welcome aboard and enjoy the flight," he said before returning to the cockpit of the plane to prepare for takeoff.

Cindy asked Don if he would like coffee or water or some other refreshment. Feeling as if he was on the proverbial cloud nine, he said he would like a bloody mary.

As the plane lifted off, Don could see over the horizon his pretty little town and he began to identify the different landmarks. The university campus was distinctive with its football stadium and classroom buildings laid out in an unmistakably organized footprint.

Up, up and away, the plane climbed quickly and smoothly. In a matter of minutes, the GPS on the TV monitor read that the altitude was 18,000 feet and speed was 320 knots. It was almost eerily quiet in the cabin and Don was feeling ten-feet tall-and successful, almost smug. He grinned as he fantasized having all of his friends see him now. Even Karen was standing in their yard down below, looking up for the plane. But it had already left the area. She said a little prayer for his safe trip. He had promised to call her once he landed in Atlantic City.

Once the plane leveled off, Cindy pulled down his tray and placed the drink in the cup holder.

Don noticed that the plastic cup had the name of the "MNS" printed on the outside of the cup. He also observed an identical carpeted MNS logo on the bulkhead wall, displaying the finite detail of their entire operation.

As the plane starts its descent into Atlantic City, Don stretched his neck to see the Atlantic Ocean. The pilot's voice suddenly interrupted his thoughts when it came on the intercom, telling Don, "Welcome to Atlantic City!" He continued his monologue that he had most likely repeated countless times to other VIP passengers, informing Don that they would fly over the city and out into the Atlantic and then do a one-eighty to line up with the runway. The airport was just 3 miles from the coast. *Wow, what a sight, all the casinos, the Board Walk, the crashing surf, the beautiful Ocean! Man, this is paradise,* Don whispers to himself!

As the plane touched ground, Don looked to the sky and mouthed a sincere "Thank you God." It'd been a great ride but more importantly to someone as inexperienced at flying as he was, a safe one. The plane taxied over to the private jet hanger and office. Cindy said, "Mr. Don, it was a pleasure serving you and have a good visit. I'll see you on the return trip." Don thanked her as he exited the craft and walked down the stairs where an overweight, bald headed man was standing at the bottom.

"Hello Don, I'm Golden, it's nice to meet you." Don was a little surprised that he would meet Golden there on the tarmac. They got into a white stretch limousine that had the printed name of the *Paradise Hotel and Casino* on each side of the Limo. They headed to the Casino which was about a fifteen-minute drive. *Wow, another nice ride.* Golden mixed up a bloody mary for himself and asked Don if he would like one. "Sure," Don replied. *After all,* he thought to himself, *I am in high roller-heaven.*

Golden congratulated Don on his latest bet and told him, "You're going to love these guys. I've have been working with this group for about five years and they have been very good to me."

Chapter 13

As they drove up to the Casino, Don noticed the name "Paradise Hotel and Casino" and Don thought it was a perfect name. The covered drop-off area for the Hotel and Casino was covered in neon lights, mirrored glass and had the feel of success! The valet opened his door and he stepped out as a group of onlookers stood gawking and asking themselves, who he might be. Somewhat embarrassed, he stood tall and pretended that riding around in limos was something he did every day.

Almost forgetting, he called Karen from his cell. "I made it, you won't have to cash in the life insurance policy." He was feeling a little too self-assured, thanks to the drink.

"Not funny," Karen said, "but I am relieved, thanks for calling. How as the trip?"

"Great! I wish you'd been with me."

"Well, stay in touch and behave yourself. I love you."

"I will, don't worry. I love you, too." *I can handle myself. After all, I have a lot of respect for myself.*

As Don entered the Hotel he was greeted by a tall, thin woman.

"Hello Don, my name is Sally O'Brian. I will be your host for the next couple of days." She was about 5'6", blond hair, sharp figure and dressed in a baby blue business suit and high heels. She was certainly attractive and well spoken.

Feeling more important by the moment, Don replied, "it's nice meeting you Sally, I will certainly need someone to help me through these next couple of days."

"I will show you to your room. Your bags are being taken to your room. How was the flight?" she asked. Her inquiry was more automatic than curious, but Don was too busy acting like a seasoned pro to notice.

"Well, that is one nice plane and the ride was smooth!"

Sally, leading the way, informed him that the schedule called for a luncheon where Don would meet the group and begin to understand his role in what they wanted from their project.

Don followed obediently behind Sally into the elevator and she punched "9" on the panel. When they arrived on the hotel's ninth floor, she led him to the end of the hallway, where she opened the door to his Suite 908.

He was blown away at what he saw when he entered. The floor to ceiling, ten-foot glass spanned the entire living area and the view of the Atlantic Ocean was breath taking. His first thought was, *Wow, I've got to bring Karen here, she would love this.* he noticed the red velvet, floor to ceiling drapes, the wrap-around balcony, the huge kitchen, bar area, and the island which framed the room.

This is not a room; it's a huge apartment in the sky overlooking the great Atlantic Ocean. Sally showed Don his bedroom and bath. Again, this is a five-star set up: huge bed, floor to ceiling glass overlooking the Ocean, huge bathroom with all the right amenities – granite counter tops, marble floor, mirrors on every wall, super lighting and a walk-in steam shower with an old fashion tub next to it. All shiny gold fixtures which added elegance to the whole room. "I don't know what I've done to deserve this, but it sure is nice," he mumbled almost inaudibly, as if talking to himself.

"You are going to like the group," she said. "They are top shelf in everything they do."

Chapter 14

She left with instructions for Don to come to the second floor in half an hour in the Atlantis Room. "You'll meet everyone there and have a great lunch," she said, handing him a small menu and suggesting that he put in his order so the food would be ready when they all sat down for lunch.

"What do you recommend?" he asked.

"I usually get the lobster rolls and a chardonnay."

“That sounds great, I’ll have the same.”

As she left, Sally said that it would be an informal lunch and that a golf shirt with a sport coat would appropriate.

As he prepared to leave for lunch, he stopped in the foyer and took a look at himself in in the floor to ceiling mirror on the wall. Standing erect, he stood up straight and sucked in his stomach. *Well Donnie boy, the good Lord is certainly shining down on you. This could be the start of a new and exciting chapter of your life, one that could put the Williamses on the map.*

Looking sharp in his navy-blue blazer, tan pants and light brown lace-up shoes, he left his suite feeling confident and self-assured. After all he has just arrived in a jet, a limousine and now leaving a five-Star Suite on the Atlantic Ocean to attend a luncheon where new clients would be waiting.

On the elevator, he inadvertently pressed the third-floor button but then remembers it was the second floor. The elevator stopped at the third floor. When no one got on, he continued down a floor. When the door opened, he heard voices from down the hallway to his left. He stepped out and looked to his left and at the end of the hallway he caught sight of a group of men entering what appears to be the Atlantis room.

He walked in and was immediately greeted by Sally. It was a nice, if contrived gesture, designed to make him feel comfortable. The room was beautiful and large. Twelve-foot ceilings with more floor-to-ceiling glass windows that looked out on the Atlantic Ocean. The windows were adorned with navy blue curtains. Matching navy-blue spotless carpet with gold medallions evenly spaced graced the floor. A beautiful chandelier and wall sconces completed the décor. A huge Walnut conference table and a full kitchen with a huge island added to the entire environment. Everything he had seen literally screamed opulence. Observers with more subdued tastes might even call it gawdy and ostentatious, but those descriptive adjectives never occurred to Don.

Sally grabbed his hand and led him over to a group of men who were chatting busily in the center of the room. "Gentleman, this is Mr. Don Williams." They all greeted and welcomed him to the Hotel. The first man to extend his hand to Don hand was a short, but a well-built man.

"Hello, Don, my name is Fred Chicky, I'm the General Manager of the Hotel and Casino. I hope you found everything to your liking."

"Yes, sir, Mr. Chicky, very nice and thank you."

"We're very informal here and we only use first names, so Fred is perfect."

A tall, six-foot-two, tanned, black haired man stepped up next. "Hello Don, my name is Dee Lombart. I'm owner and president of our savings and loan and development group. We're so pleased to meet you and spend some time with you. We are excited at the possibility of working with you on some of our upcoming projects. Welcome abord and please make yourself comfortable here."

"Hello, Don, my name is William T. Smith. You can call me Billy. I'm the project manager for all of our group's developments. You and I will be working together when we work out a schedule that we hope fits yours." Billy was short and a little overweight for his height but he seemed pleasant and Don thought he would be easy to work with.

Introductions were coming faster than he could possibly remember all the names and faces were already beginning to run together.

Seeming to see Don's growing confusion, Dee interrupted to say, "Let's all sit down and have a nice lunch. There're name tags on the table to help you remember everyone's name. You're seated next to Sally. I bet you can remember *her* name." That drew laughter from everyone except Don, who could only smile wanly.

Dee asked everyone to bow their heads as he blesses the meal. It was a gesture Don appreciated and he immediately started to feel more than a little comfortable with this group. Dee then announced that there would be no discussion of business at the lunch, adding the caveat: at 9:00 a.m. the next day, in the same where they were enjoying their repast, there would be breakfast and a short presentation by Billy on the group's upcoming projects following by a general discussion among all those present.

The meal was served in short order and the lobster rolls were devoured. The cold chardonnay went down easily. The conversation stayed about sports and how well the sports book was doing. Fred handed Don a small leather bag filled with ten ohe-hundred-dollar casino chips. "Don," he said, "I believe Sally and you are going to dinner tonight with Golden. When you get back, you can bet with these chips because we want you to have a good time as our guest and win if you can."

"Stick close to Sally in the Casino," Dee added. "She is a pro and can make some good bets for you."

"Where is my bag, Fred?" Sally asked.

"Shucks, Sally, I thought you would never ask," Fred replied as he handed Sally. "It's the usual," he said.

Following the lunch, they all said goodbye, adding that they were looking forward to seeing Don the next morning.

Chapter 15

Sally escorted Don to the elevator and informed him that they were to meet in the Lobby at 5:45 that afternoon. The limo, she said, would take them to Spanky's a favorite steak house along the coast. Then, after dinner, they would hit the tables and try to win a little of the casino money. They would be joined by Golden, who she said was a good friend of Spanky. As they part, Sally told Don that the dress was informal and that if he preferred, he could wear jeans and a sport coat.

Don awakened at 4:00 p.m. from a two- hour nap and called Karen to let her know that everything was going well. He described all the amenities and he told her how nice and professional his hosts were and that they were going to take him to a nice steak house.

Karen asked a curious – and ominous – question: "Don't you wonder what they want you to do and at what price? Have they given you any indication?"

"Well, Karen, I'm a big boy and only a contractor. So, if I stay in my lane, so to speak, and do what I do best, we should be okay."

They talked a little longer and Karen finally told Don she loved him and to call later and let her know how the night went.

"I love you too and I will call when I get in, probably around 10:00 tonight. Good bye, baby."

Don jumped into a steaming hot shower to clean up for the night. Fortunately, he had brought a pair of tan blue jeans and with his black golf shirt and his dark sport coat, he figured he would fit in just fine.

Don arrived in the lobby at 5:40 p.m. and Sally and Golden were already there. They watched as Gino, the Limo driver, opened the Lobby doors and led them to the beautiful white, stretch limo. Golden jumped in first and sat in the seat behind the driver while Sally and Don sat facing Golden towards the front of the vehicle.

There was a small ice chest in the middle of the floor board and Golden immediately asked if anyone wanted cocktail, saying that he was going to have a Scotch.

Sally asked if there was a Prosecco available as Golden opened the top of the ice chest. She already knew there was since she phoned Gino an hour earlier and told him to stock her drink in ice the chest. Golden said, "You are in luck and there is even a champagne glass for you." He poured Don a handsome two ounces with one ice cube as well as himself.

Sally said they were about ten minutes from Spanky's, "so y'all relax." Golden told Don how good a friend Spanky was to him and Sally. The Paradise sent a lot of business to Spanky "and he's most appreciative." Everything felt like a celebration and everyone was in a good mood. Don, once again, wondered what he did to deserve all of this.

When they arrived at Spanky's, Gino stopped the car and walked around to open the door for the trio. Don noticed that the Restaurant was built on top of structural columns high above the beach. The Restaurant was a wood-clad building and was painted to appear like old driftwood. A huge neon sign on top of roof spells out, "SPANKY'S." The sign not only lit up the parking lot, but one could see it from almost half-a-mile away.

They walked into a small lobby and took an elevator up to the Restaurant. As they walked into the restaurant, a large round man walked up to Golden and embraced him a huge bear hug, difficult task in itself, given both of their expanded belly's, but they do their best. It was evident that theirs was a close relationship.

Spanky immediately grabbed Sally's arm and kisses her hand. "It's great to see you and who is this handsome man?" As he posed the question, he was already reaching out to shake Don's hand.

"This is a special member of my gang from New York and he is down here to talk some business," Golden said. "Don Williams, this is Spanky."

"Well, Don," Spanky said before Don could say anything, "it's nice to meet you and hope you have a successful trip. Follow me, I have you seated at my best table."

Don took in the surroundings. It was a beautiful restaurant. It has the driftwood feel to it, huge glass windows overlooking the Ocean, stark white table cloths, navy blue cushion chairs and a glass enclosed candle on every table. It was all quite seductive, including the aroma coming from the open kitchen adjoining the seating area. The Kitchen was partially closed off by glass partitions, but one could still see the flames on the open pit as steaks are being prepared.

As they were seated next to the window overlooking the ocean, Don also noticed the tiki lanterns with their flames flitting down on the beach, creating a resort type feel. He also observed several yachts moored about half-a-mile off shore with their cabin lights outlining the shape of the crafts. It was not quite sunset, but the western sun was setting and as they looked east, they can see the white billowing clouds being drenched by the sun. The sky is a brilliant silver blue and the overall view could not have been more spectacular.

An attractive young lady approached and welcomed them to the restaurant. Her name was Ruby. She asked if anyone would like to start with a cocktail and everyone all ordered the same drinks they'd had in the Limo. "I'll get those right away while you guys look at the menu," she said with a smile that revealed perfect, gleaming teeth.

Spanky literally rolled up in what appeared to be a huge, motorized high chair on wheels. It is wide and high enough for Spanky to sit comfortably at the table with us. He used it to get around table to table in the restaurant to speak with his guests as they enjoyed their meals. It made sense; when one owned his own restaurant, nothing looked out of place.

"So, Don," he said, "we have the best steaks on the coast. I have them shipped in daily from my vendor in Iowa."

Golden said, "Don, on the weekends, you cannot get a table here, unless you call way ahead for a reservation. The whole dining experience here is that good."

Spanky went over the selection of steaks as if his guests were unable to read the menu for themselves. "The sixteen-ounce rib eye, the eight-ounce filet and the prime rib are to die for," he gushed.

As the group discussed their selections, Sally asked Spanky if he had a couple bottles of Silver Oak Cabernet on hand. "Sally, I always know when you are coming. Of course I do!"

Ruby soon arrived with the drinks and the group ordered: Sally, a Filet, Golden and Don, sixteen-ounce rib eyes. Completing the order were a small salad, and a baked potato for all.

When the orders arrived, Ruby opened the wine and poured it into a Canter to let it breathe. Hardly anyone spoke because the food was too delicious for conversation. Spanky again rolled up to the table and asked if the steaks are cooked properly. The diners could only nod their heads and mumble "Yes."

The wine was smooth and its taste had a good beginning and a great ending as it was consumed. *This is heaven, just perfect. Karen would be so impressed!* When the meal was finished, a small bowl of "bread pudding" with a small scoop of vanilla ice cream was served.

At the end of the meal, they thanked Spanky. He said, "Glad you enjoyed it. Don when you come back to town, bring the missus down, would love to meet her."

In the Limo, Don asked Golden how Spanky got his name. Golden smiled and told Don that Spanky won a New Jersey Lottery worth over $750,000. The winnings gave him enough money to buy the land where the Restaurant sat and Spanky became a frequent customer at the strip clubs in Atlantic City. He threw money around like there was no end. He was a big tipper and would place $100 bills in the girls G string! He then thought – correctly, it turned out – that he could spank them on the butt for his generous tip. They would all line up to get spanked when he began his pet hobby.

"It seems to fit his personality," Don said, laughing. "He's a very outgoing man."

Chapter 16

BACK TO THE CASINO

On the ride back to the casino, there was minimal conversation, though Don did express how excellent the whole experience was. Golden informed Don that Spanky was his biggest client and bet up to $25,000 a game. So the night's $750 meal was comped. Golden continued, saying that Spanky bet a hundred thousand dollars on the previous year's Super Bowl and won. "I wish the meal was twice that amount," he said.

Don is astonished that one person would – or could – gamble such an amount.

Sally said that they are going to gamble Fred's money and win a little more. "Sally, I have never gambled in a casino before," Don said.

"Just stick close to me and will guide you, it'll be a lot of fun, you'll see."

"I'm going to the sports book to check the latest odds for this weekend's game," Golden said. "Let's all go their first, Sally. I want Don to see what happens behind the curtain, so to speak."

She agrees. When they arrive at the lobby of the hotel, they all walk to the Sports Book. The sports book is inside the casino but tucked away behind a curved wall separated from sight and sound.

As they turn the corner, Don could feel the space and is thrown for a minute. "Wow, he said, almost whispering, this is like a giant arcade." He noticed the huge LED TVs that had to be twelve feet in diameter - three of them stretched across one wall, high above what seemed to be metal cages, which he leaned soon enough were the betting windows. There were six additional smaller TVs, if you can imagine the word smaller to describe sets that were eight feet in diameter, draped on each side of the large TVs, three on each side, stacked on top of each other.

He then observed several large screens with green numbers and orange names next to the numbers. Golden explained that those screens were what were called the "odds boards." Everything in the world one would like to bet was up there, he said – pro football, college football, pro and college basketball, hockey, major league baseball, soccer, tennis and prop bets which are individual bets for teams and players in all sports.

The horse racing odds were shown at the time of the races and were featured on the TV screen as the race occurred. There was a separate betting window for horse racing since the action moves quicker than any other sport.

In the middle of the huge brightly lit room were rows of seating with nice chairs and betting stations with a desk top stretched from one end of the room to the other. At each chair, was a small TV where the bettor can watch his individual wager. Accordingly, it made sense that a comfortable bettor could become a bigger bettor, which is always good for the house. The casino made a huge profit from the sports book.

"Well, your Bears are playing the Giants and are getting 6.5 points this weekend," Golden said. "You don't have to drive here just to bet, that's why I'm here. You just call me from the comfort of your home."

"yep I get it now," Don answered.

"Okay, Don, let's get to the tables," Sally interrupted, pulling him away.

On the way, they stopped by the bar and grabbed another drink, just to keep loose. Golden said that he would stay in the sports book and get his odds for the weekend games. "Good luck, he chirped as they walked away.

Walking into the casino was like being transported into a world of energy. Bright lights, bells ringing, people excited and a huge room with dozens of Slot Machines, Table Games and young, attractive, sharply dressed waitresses walking around delivering drinks to the players. Don is blown away. He had never witnessed an event center like this. He felt the rush of money being won and lost. One could tell that the clientele is serious about spending their time here just by observing their mien. The fact is it was a different world far removed from the everyday life that Don had lived.

The first stop in the casino was the blackjack table. It was a semi-circle table with 5 chairs facing the Dealer. "Let's sit down and bring out Fred's money," Sally said. They sat side by side as he noticed that she had taken the first seat on the left. She said that the seat's position is known as "first base" and she could better help him by being the first one to determine the dealer's hand. Don had no clue but who was he to question this strategy?

Don took out his little leather bag with the ten one-hundred-dollar chips. Sally instructed him to give the dealer three chips and ask to change it into twenty-five-dollar chips. Don noticed that the smaller chips were green and the number "25" was stamped in the center of the chip.

The blackjack table was covered with a green soft velvet top and he noticed that there are small imprinted white circles situated in front of each chair. He soon learned that this was where players placed their bets in order for the dealer to deal them their hands.

Don also noted that there was what is called a "shoe." A clear plastic box shaped like a shoe. All of the cards to be dealt come from the shoe as the dealer will swipe his hand at the base of the shoe to deal the cards. Since they were the first customers, the dealer took out three decks of cards and spread the cards face up. He moved all of the cards in a random fashion, mixing them in a variety of ways. He then picked all of them up with his two hands and molded them into three stacks, face down, and hand shuffled each stack of cards. Then, he took a card from each stacked deck of cards and handed the card to Sally. She placed it into the middle of the stack. He then placed that stack of cards into the shoe and repeated it two more times.

Now it was time to deal, so place your bets! Sally bet one hundred dollars and told Don to bet two green chips, or fifty dollars. It was just the two of them at the table and Sally loved that. She could control Don's bet as she saw the cards come out.

The dealer reaches for the first card and he dealt Sally a card, face down. Same for Don, face down. Then he dealt himself a card, again face down. The second card Sally received was face up and it was an eight. Don receives a second card face up and it was a ten. Dealer gives himself a card face up, a three.

Sally, loved that he has a three. It gave both her and Don an early advantage because the dealer had a long way to go to get to twenty-one. The hand nearest to the total of twenty-one wins. Sally looked at her first card, the one that was face down, and saw that it was a Jack, which, like all face cards, counted as ten. In most cases, a face card is good unless you go "bust" by going over twenty-one. That's not good.

Sally waved her hand over the chips signaling that she was good with her total of eighteen. Don, a little nervous, looked at his first card and it is a nine. He showed it to her and she told him to wave his hand over his chips because he was also good with your total of nineteen.

The dealer must take a card if he has a total of sixteen and he has to stand on seventeen and cannot take another card. The odds makers know that a player will likely bust if he takes a card after reaching seventeen. So, they are hoping the dealer will do the busting on his own.

The dealer turned over his first card which was face down and it was a five, leaving at a total of eight. He had to draw another card and it was a nine, for a total of seventeen. He had to stay put. Both Sally and Don had totals nearer to twenty-one than the dealer which meant Sally won one hundred dollars and Don won fifty.

I like this game, an elated Don thought. "Let it ride," he heard Sally say to him, meaning he should bet one hundred dollars. She did the same, wagering two hundred on the next deal. The cards came out and Sally was sitting on a four and a ten, a total of fourteen. Don had a king and a nine, a total of nineteen. The dealer had an ace showing and that wasn't good for either of the two players. He next turned a seven. An ace can be either a one or eleven. He chose the eleven, giving him eighteen total. Sally waved her hand toward her and the Dealer hands her a 5!! What luck! She and Don both have nineteen. They both win again.

The game continued and to Don's surprise – and delight - after about thirty minutes he had accumulated $450 and Sally, well over a thousand dollars. It was a bad night for the house on that blackjack table.

"Where are we going now?" Don asked.

"We're going to play craps," she answered. Don has no clue, but decided she was doing great so far, so why not? Craps is a dice game. It got its name from when the thrower ended his or her dice throw by rolling a seven before the he or she hit the number that they rolled on the "come out" roll.

As they walked over to the table, Don saw that there were a number of people surrounding a huge table and they are all looking down into what is described as a pit. It is almost like looking down into a canyon with about 1 foot of depth from the top of the edge of the table down to the flat floor of the table where the dice are thrown. He also saw that there were no chairs around the table except for the one person dressed in a suit sitting in the middle of the table with a whole bunch of chips in front of him. He must be the *captain* of this ship!

Directly across from the captain was a man with a stick. With the stick, he gathered the dice and then shuttles them to the person throwing the dice.

Green velvet again covered the area where the dice are thrown and many white numbers and boxes filled with numbers that are scattered all over this flat playing ground. There was a railing around the top of the table forty-two inches off the floor where the bettor keeps his chips in a tray designed to hold them in an organized fashion.

Sally found an opening around the table where she and Don could fit in and start to gamble. There were a couple of dealers next to the captain. They handled the bets, both collecting and paying the customer. Sally explained to Don that the "white puck" signals that there is a new player throwing the dice and that is known as "coming out"! That is when bets are placed before the player throws.

Sally instructed Don to do exactly what she did and bet with twenty-five-dollar chips while she would bet with one hundred-dollar chips. Their table was a twenty-five-dollar minimum bet table and normally serious gamblers played at this level. Sally placed one of her chips on the "field," a large rectangular area where a player wins if the dice hit any one of the numbers, two, three, four, nine, ten, eleven, or twelve. She also placed a hundred on the number five which covers her bet if the number five is rolled instead of the other numbers in the field. Don did exactly as she did with his twenty-five-dollar chips. Her bet was for one roll only. Therefore, she would win or lose after the dice are tossed on this one roll.

She told him that the odds are slanted toward the house on her bet – sixteen ways to win, twenty-four ways to lose. In all of her experiences of playing this bet, however it always amazed her how many times this bet is a winner. In fact, she has witnessed the field bet winning three to four times in a row.

The player rolled a nine. They won on the field bet but lost on the five, since she called that the five was working on the *come-out* roll. She let her winnings ride on the field. Now, she bet two hundred dollars and Don bet fifty on the next roll. No more five this time so, she placed the two hundred on that nine will be rolled before the seven. If she is correct, she is paid 1.5 to one or she wins $150.

The player threw the dice again and luck struck! He rolls a nine. "Winner, winner, chicken dinner!" she screamed as she won two hundred on the field bet and $150 on placing the nine – a total of $350 winnings. Don won fifty dollars on the field bet and seventy-five on the nine for total winnings of $125.

It appeared that it was a good night at the craps table as Sally worked her way alternately betting with and against the player. Betting against the player is known as the "don't pass" bet, meaning that if the player rolls a six, for instance, and rolls a seven before rolling a six again, one wins the "don't pass" bet.

Sally knew that on average, the seven hits about every four to six rolls. The "don't pass" bet can be profitable when the table goes cold, meaning in turn that the players who are rolling are not hitting their "come out" number consistently. If one bets the "don't pass" on the "come out" roll and the roll is a seven or eleven, then he or she loses the bet. Sally always threw out a "Yo" bet on the "Come Out" roll. If the Player rolls an eleven, then the "yo" bet pays 15 to 1. She usually bet twenty-five dollars on the one time "yo" bet. Twenty-five multiplied by fifteen is a $375 pay out. That covered her usual $200 to $300 bet on the "don't pass" bet.

Chapter 17

Don followed Sally all night. The woman appeared to have the magic touch. Sh was a master at knowing the game, balancing her bets against each other. After about an hour, Don had accumulated at least $4,000 in black chips and Sally at least $9,000 in black chips.

She announced that she was ready to "color up." She places all of her chips in the middle of the table where the dealer stacked and told her how much the stack held in dollars. He then converted the black chips into $500 chips to make it easier to carry to the "payout window." In all casinos, the payout window will be located in a faraway corner in order to make it as difficult as possible to cash in your chips for cash. The casinos do this by design in the hope that players will stop along the way and gamble some of that money away, hoping that greed will seduce them. The ploy works more often than not.

Sally had won $9,350 and Don's take was $5,560 - including Fred's gambling gift to them. All in all, it was a wonderful night! Don was exhausted so, Sally suggested a night cap. As they made their way to a quiet table in the lounge around the corner from the casino, Don thanked Sally for the most entertaining night of his life and for the great education in gambling. Sally cautioned him, saying, "It doesn't always work out that way. Gambling is fickle. Winning at the tables is all about units, meaning you keep your bets constant. If you start losing, never, ever "chase" your money by doubling or tripling your bets. That's why they give you free drinks in order to loosen you up so that you lose discipline. It works every time. That's how they can pay for this beautiful edifice."

They talked a little longer before finally leaving the lounge, hopping into the Limo that was standing by while they played and headed to the Hotel. Sally inquired of Golden's whereabouts and Gino said he took him back to the Hotel about an hour earlier.

At the Hotel, they headed for the elevators. Sally, who was staying on the sixth floor, exited first. As she did so, she turned and gave Don a big hug and said, "I'm so glad you are going to be on the team. You're going to make some money for you and your family. See you at 9:00 tomorrow morning."

Don entered his room exhausted. A lot had been packed into his day – a jet ride, meeting the Company Brass, dinner at Spanky's, casino gambling as if he had money – just too much for one day.

It was about 9:30 p.m. when he called Karen to wish her a good night. They exchanged brief pleasantries but he purposely neglected to tell her about his winnings at the casino. When they hung up, he undressed and plopped down on the bed and almost instantly fell asleep with a satisfied smile on his face. His last naïve thought was *I must be somebody!*

He awoke around 7:30 a.m. and immediately hit the shower, shaved and dressed for the morning's meeting. Full of anticipation, his choice of wardrobe was dress pants, a long sleeve dress shirt, dress shoes and his sport coat. Looking every bit the professional businessman, he headed down a little early for the 9:00 a.m. breakfast meeting.

Although fully fifteen minutes early, he was surprised when he walks into the room to find that everyone was already there. "Well, here's our big winner!" Dee's voice boomed over the din of the restaurant. Everyone in the group started to clapping. Hotel staff members working in the room, realizing he had succeeded in a big way at the tables and taking their cue from the hotel and casino executives, spontaneously joined in the applause. Sally, obviously, had let them know of their lucrative night.

Don, somewhat embarrassed but nonetheless loving the attention, acknowledged the compliment. "

well had it not been for Sally's coaching, I would have been out of there real quick." Fred, the Casino Manager, said, "Don, we're thrilled you had a good night. We're so glad you got to benefit from the experience of a pro gambler like Sally."

Don feeling indebted to his hosts, reached into his pocket and pulled out the ten one-hundred-dollar bills to repay the stake that Fred had given him the day before but Fred would have none of it. He waved the money away, telling Don to just accept the gift as part of his "appearance fee" for joining the group.

"Are you sure?"

"Absolutely. We hope you will become family."

"Well, gee, that is awfully nice of you."

Dee interrupted the awkward exchange to tell everyone to grab a plate and head to the breakfast buffet. Don loaded his tray down with scrambled eggs, bacon, fruit and a large glass of orange Juice – *just the right breakfast to cure a slight hangover.*

Don couldn't help but notice that they had set up a large projection screen across from the big table where they were seated. He also observed the Projector tied in with a computer that doubtless held the information that he is so eagerly waiting to hear. Dee again asked everyone to bow their heads and he delivers a soft and earnest prayer. Don was feeling comfortable around this group, especially since the night before when he had enjoyed a great dinner with Golden and Sally and followed that with the great fun he had with his first experience with casino gambling.

Chapter 18

The conversation during breakfast was light and casual as Sally regaled the others with a recap of their gambling experience. She complimented Fred on the well-run casino and especially the friendly staff that handled everything in an efficient and professional manner. It was a well-rehearsed and often repeated spiel and Fred thanked her for the compliment. He announced that they are expecting a big weekend with about 200 retirees coming in from New York on six large tourist buses. "The hotel and will be full and our restaurants will do great as well." *Wow, what a great way to capture cash flow*, Don thinks to himself.

Sally, smiling, asked only partly in jest, "Fred, do you have enough slot machines?" It's common knowledge that slots are the favorite among elderly gamblers who seem enamored with just sitting and watching and listening the machines as they whirl toward a possible winning payout for the player.

Fred smiled at Sally's levity and said that they had recently added another wing to the casino exclusively for slot machines and especially designed for that clientele. "We've given them panoramic views of the Ocean, their own buffet, bar and rest rooms – all in the same area," he said. "It'll make them feel very special!" Don's hosts laughed in appreciation of Fred's foresight even though they knew full well the wing had been planned and constructed long before anyone knew of the retirees' visit.

As they finished breakfast and the table was cleared by the staff, coffee was served as the lights were dimmed. Dee arose to initiate the presentation. He again thanked Don for coming to hear about MNS's business and also complimented all of the other officers in attendance for their hard work and care for making the company successful before picking up the remote to the Power Point presentation.

The first slide displayed the MNS logo and its organization chart: Chairman of the Board Dee, hotel and casino General Manager Fred, Project Manager William Smith, and a host of other names that Don didn't recognize because he had not yet met them. His preliminary introductions had been limited to the corporation's heavy hitters.

The second slide illustrated the different entities that MNS was involved in. Don slowly took in the names of those entities: D.L. Savings and Loan, Paradise Casino and Hotel, MNS Development Company, MNS Sports Book, and MNS Financial Group. He also learned for the first time that Sally O'Brian was the corporate attorney for all the entities. He was impressed with the latter revelation with the realization that she handled all the companies' agreements and contracts. *So, I guess she will be my main contact if all this goes forward.*

Dee began with the "D.L. Savings and Loan" and told the group that the good news was that last quarter, the savings and loan had amassed over $1.8 billion dollars in assets and was projected to reach $2 billion the following year. The numbers were staggering to Don: *This is a huge business.* As Dee outlined the rest of the portfolio, Don remained transfixed. *No wonder they have a jet plane and a casino and a huge Development company!*

Dee, wrapping up his presentation, called up William Smith, the development company's project manager. "Finally, Don, this is why you're here," he said. "We hope to convince you to join our construction and development team. We have three projects we'd like to present to you for your consideration.

A click of the remote and a slide was projected onto the screen that revealed architectural delineations of the projects in full color and they looked beautiful. "They're all located in Newark, about a two-hour-drive from your home. The first project is a 40,000-square-foot, four-story office building. The estimated project cost is around eight million dollars. The second one is a 60,000-square-foot, three-story store and lock facility, estimated project cost is $10.5 million, and the third project is a one hundred twenty-unit, luxury apartment complex estimated at $12 million. Don quickly added up the total project dollars and he estimated $30.5 million dollars.

"So, Don,' continued Smith, "the way we work is that we would like for you to perform as the construction manager. What that entails simply is that we want you to run the job, including staying on budget, building on the timeline projected, and delivering a quality product. The good news is that we already have a team of subcontractors. We're comfortable with them and and their prices. We're open to your getting prices from some of your subs and any other folks who can help us get the job done."

"You will need to hire three superintendents. I have a list of possible people you can set up interviews with. They all live in the Newark vicinity, which will make it easy for them to get to the jobs. In addition, Williams LLC, my construction company will pull permits, make all payroll and carry all necessary insurance coverages. Again, your job will be to construct the job, on time and on budget."

"Well, that's very enticing," Don said, at a temporary loss of what else to say about this sudden potential windfall about to be dropped into his lap. "Can you tell me what kind of fee I'll make?"

Dee, taking the question as his cue, stepped in to say, "Sally handles all of our agreements and details. That's why she will ride with you back to Empire after the meeting here where she'll go over the projects in greater detail. And I might add Don, we will ask you to sign a NDA, (non-disclosure agreement) as we like to keep our business private."

"I have no problems with that," said Don, who was familiar with NDAs as an integral part of doing business. "That sounds good. I feel comfortable with Sally since we spent a night together making a little money." Everyone laughed at his Freudian slip and he was momentarily embarrassed. As the meeting ended, Don shook hands with each of the partners. Each one said they hoped he would come on board. He thanked everyone for the great hospitality and walked out with Sally.

Sally said, "Well, Don pack up, we'll meet downstairs in thirty minutes and take off about forty-five minutes after that."

Don agreed and headed to his room to pack, which was not much. Arriving in his room, he looked out over the Atlantic Ocean, glistening so bright into the eastern morning sun. He sat on the bed and pondered his good fortune for a moment. He was going over in his head the potential fees he would make on thirty million dollars of construction as a construction manager. *If it is ten percent, I make three million dollars gross. Add that to the $1.2 million fee from the basketball arena renovation, then over the next say 3 years, I should gross about $4.2 million, or approximately $1.4 million a year.* Then he recalled what he'd heard about no payroll, no insurance, no pulling permits, that he believed would be is a huge savings of time and money. Suddenly, he couldn't wait to get with Sally and get down to brass tacks.

Chapter 19

"RIDE SALLY RIDE"

Feeling pumped on the inside, he practically skipped to the elevator. He pushed the lobby button and it seemed that it was taking forever to reach the lobby. It didn't help that the elevator stopped twice to take on other occupants headed to the lobby as well.

"Good morning," he greeted his fellow passengers cheerfully. They appeared just as happy to see him as well and return the greeting. After all, they were there to have a good time and to hopefully win at the tables. As the doors opened to the Lobby, Don was so excited that he had to hold himself back and let them get off first. *Another irritating delay to getting with Sally!*

The limo was waiting for him and Gino grabbed his bag and loaded it into the trunk. Suddenly, Golden seemed to appear from nowhere. "Congratulations, I hear you may soon become a rich man soon."

"Maybe so," Don replied. Still basking in the glow of the morning's meeting, he quickly added, "I want to bet the Bears this Sunday, getting 6½ points at the Giants!" Don had $4500 in his pocket from the Casino the night before and another thousand he had in his safe from the winnings from the previous Sunday.

Golden, surprised at his sudden display of confidence, asked, "Make $1,100 to win a thousand, like last time?

Not hesitating, Don says quietly and confidently, "No, make it $5,500 to win five thousand!"

Golden grinning widely, laughed and said, "You've made my day. In fact, knowing the bright future you have, I'm going to increase your line of credit to twenty-five thousand dollars!"

Well, I think that may fit in just right. I'm getting used to this betting thing. He shook Golden's hand and walked to the limo. Sally was already inside, relaxing. They departed for the airport where Don anticipated that there were blue skies and green money ahead.

The limo drove onto the tarmac and deposited them at the plane's steps. They climbed the eight steps into the cabin where they were greeted by the same crew members: the two pilots, Ben and Jerry and the flight attendant, Cindy. Again, smartly dressed in her crisp uniform and looking sprite, Cindy chirped, "Welcome aboard" as they entered.

Let's sit across from each other," Sally suggested to Don. "That way, there's a table between us so that we can go over the agreements.

There was no argument from Don, who sat facing the back of the plane. At this point, he was just ready to learn as much about his future as quickly as possible.

They each request a glass of water from Cindy. As the plane lifts off, Don couldn't help thinking that it was a good day to fly: blue skies and good company! As the plane levels off and reaches its required altitude, Sally asked Don if he would like a bloody mary as she removed out a file folder from her briefcase and laid it on the table between them.

Before she could begin, Don, beginning to become comfortable in his new position, said, "Sally can I ask you a few questions?"

"Absolutely. Don, we're going to be working together on some very important projects and it's important we keep all lines of communication open on every level. "Let me add," she continued, "my position with this company is very powerful and I've worked hard over the last eight years to gain their trust. We have six other construction companies just like yours working with us under the same format. So far, it has worked extremely well. William Smith is great to work with. He's been doing construction for over twenty-five years and he has made a ton of money for MNS."

Don, impressed, got right to the point. "Sally, I would like to know what kind of fee will I'll be earning by doing this work."

"Don it's most generous, we believe, but before we go any further, I must get you to sign this NDA," she replied, asking Cindy to have one of the pilots come back and witness Don's signature in about 5 minutes. She went over the NDA carefully and in detail with Don, explaining to him that this protects MNS from Don's sharing any proprietary company business with anyone else.

Don wondered aloud why the NDA was so critical that his fee couldn't be discussed yet. She explained that there were many people who were envious of MNS's success because MNS had figured a way to grow their business faster than anyone else in the construction business.

She explained that the projects that he was about to build have been researched, analyzed, and a lot of time and money have been spent determining the advantageous profit centers these projects will produce. "Knowledge is power" she says, "so if our competition beats us to a site or an area where we have learned of the huge potential, then it just dilutes the market and shrinks our profit. I know Don, you would not willingly hurt MNS, but being aware of the sensitivity of our business will keep us all in good standing."

Don said he understood what she was saying and that he was ready to sign.

She handed him the original NDA and Don looked it over carefully and noticed that the last section deals with the entirety of the NDA. The last section specifically stated that any and all business of MNS was strictly confidential and any wrongful disclosure determined by MNS, "shall be" subject to litigation and appropriate damages will be assessed. Don saw no problem with that stipulation. *I'm one who will protect the team, always.*

His name was already typed below the line so, in the presence of witnesses Cindy and one of the pilots, he signed the NDA. He was asked to sign two more NDAs, making 3 originals. Once he had signed all three, Cindy and the Pilot signed the witness lines. Sally signed her name as the notary and then clamped her seal on each signed document. She handed Don one original and kept the other two.

“Thank you, Don, and now let’s get down to business.” She removed another folder with three agreements which described the duties and responsibilities of the three projects William Smith discussed at breakfast. He carefully read through each section and it was basic boilerplate material, straightforward as discussed. The agreements, in fact, were short and simple. Don, who had read literally hundreds of contracts that were similar to the documents he was holding over his business career, was quick to see a blank line where the fee should have been typed in. He asks again what his fee was and Sally said, “Well, first Don, before we get to that, these are your copies for you to take to your attorney and have him them look them over for your sake. We don’t want to rush you but within two to three weeks, we need to button this up. So, take them to your attorney for his comments and my contact info is on the bottom of the agreements for any questions.”

“Good deal, but Sally, I would really like to know what my incentive is to be.”

Sally smiled sweetly and dropped the bomb on him: “Don, that is for me and you to negotiate!”

Don couldn’t believe it! *I can negotiate my fee! It’s not determined yet!* “Alright, let’s do this!” What he had no way of knowing was that Sally was approved to offer 14 percent, a number Don would have jumped at.

Sally cooly said, “Don, I suggest before we get started, we toast each other with our drink.” She had no sooner suggested a drink than Cindy, right on cue, set two bloody Marys in front of them and removed the coffee cups. In the back of his mind, Don though Cindy’s attentive gesture was just a little too smooth but he said nothing.

Instead, he merely smiled and held up his glass to toast Sally. *What a woman; so good looking, classy and cool all at the same time.* "Well here goes nothing, he said cheerfully."

Sally laughed as their glasses clinked. "Don, throw out a number. The number we agree on will represent the percentage fee of the gross amount of the project. For instance, since we are using $30 million as our gross amount and if we agree on three percent, then your company will receive $900,000 for its work." She was looking him straight in the eye when she said it, without of hint of joking.

Don tried hard not to flinch or show any emotion over the three percent number. He took another drink to conceal his reaction.

"Don, let me hear from you, what do you think is fair?"

"Sally, I do have a number in mind and it's ten percent."

It was Sally's turn to slow things down by taking a sip of her own drink while signaling Cindy to bring another round. It was a well-practiced and long-perfected negotiating tactic. "Don, we have never worked with you before and we could not possibly do ten percent. My number is six percent.

That's better. Now I'm looking at $1.8 million – a nice number but I believe I can do better. His drink is still on the table and Sally has finished her first and already on her second. He takes another drink. "Sally, I want ten, you say six. How about we split the baby. Can you go with eight?"

Sally eased her drink halfway to the table and holding the glass in both hands, looked straight ahead to the front of the plane and went silent for what seemed like an eternity to Don. It was a practiced ploy to act as though one had been pushed into a corner. Don, to buy time looked out the window, enjoying the rush of negotiations, but anxious at the prospect of having to accept less than he wanted or having the entire deal collapse at 28,000 feet in a Gulfstream with a powerful woman. Who in the world am I? *Am I being mentally crushed by the enormity of what I could have versus what I could lose?* "OK, Ok," he suddenly blurted, looking straight at her, I can do seven. That is fair." He could feel his pulse quicken.

Sally took another drink and continued several more seconds without speaking. Don, distracted by her beauty, the alcohol, and the VIP treatment he'd received, never once considered that he was at a huge disadvantage of negotiating with pro like Sally. Extending her hand across the table, she finally said, "You drive a hard bargain! I'm going to fill in the amount now."

Yes! I stood up to her and I'm getting 7% or $2.1 million!

Sally held the contract down with her left hand as she wrote in the number. Don can barely conceal his excitement because once she writes that number, his fee was locked in. She deftly turned the page over so that her hand covered the number as he hastily signed the document. "Don, you're a tough negotiator," she said, smiling. "Let's toast one more time to you coming aboard."

As hey finished their second drinks, Sally waves Cindy over again. Like clockwork, Cindy delivered two more bloody Marys.

Sally then handed the page with the number on it to Don who slowly looked at the number on the page. He looked at it once, then twice and then looked up at Sally and uncharacteristically said, "Are you shitting me!?"

She burst out laughing, saying, "Don, forgive me, I needed some excitement in my life and I used you, please forgive me. But yes, we're going to pay you fourteen percent. But you will earn every penny and we will get a quality job out of your firm."

Don mentally calculated $4.2 million in gross fees! *Yikes, I'm dreaming!* Even as he was fantasizing about his good fortune, the pilot announced their approach to Empire. Visibly shaken, he said to Sally, "You've become one of the best people I have ever met." It was the liquor talking but he didn't care. "If I weren't married, I'd kiss you right now and hell, I might even marry you." She laughed and pointed out that he would have to ask her first.

Chapter 20

The plane landed and came to a stop. They both stood, though it wasn't easy because they were both a little wobbly. They hugged briefly and Don grabbed the folders and exited the plane, bidding good-bye to Cindy, Ben and Jerry as he did so. He looked back once more at Sally and said, "See you soon and thanks for everything!"

His bag is brought to his car in the parking lot by the attendant at Chesters. Sitting in the driver's seat, he felt numb all over and slightly intoxicated from the combined effects of the alcohol and the contract lying on the seat next to him. He laid his head back against the head rest and tried to collect his wits. Suddenly, his cell phone rang. "Hey, you okay?" It was Karen. *What a beautiful voice.*

"Yes, I'm safe on the ground, great trip; how are you? Everything okay at home?"

"Everything's good here. I'm glad your back. A great trip?"

"Yes, very good. Honey I'm going to call the office and pick up a sandwich at Vinney's, then head home. I'm exhausted.

"Okay, be careful."

What a beautiful woman, what a beautiful life. Don Williams, you are something else. Just be careful driving.

"DECOMPRESSION"

He remained sitting in his car for about ten minutes before deciding that he could handle the short drive to Vinney's. He called the office and because it was almost noon, Matte answered the phone. "Good morning, Matte. I thought you might be at lunch."

"just about to grab a sandwich, how was the trip?"

"Couldn't have gone better." They engaged in brief small talk before Don said, "Matte, I need you to set up a meeting with attorney Jim Lewis. I need to go over some documents with him. Try to get him to come to the office tomorrow morning around 11:00 or Monday morning

Matte said she'd get right on it and let him know when Lewis confirmed. "That would be great," Don said.

Chapter 21

Don was eager to get to Vinney's to grab a sandwich and a big glass of water. Then he'd head home to recover from the last glorious forty-eight hours. When he entered into Vinney's he was greeted by his son Mark. "You off of work or school?"

Work, for a couple of hours, Mark said, "then back to class at 3:00 p.m."

Don understood and didn't waste any time as Mark ordered a patty melt and fries and water. "I'll do the same," Don told the waiter.

As they grabbed a high-top table, Mark began telling Don about some obscure "goal rigging" scheme from up in Canada. "They caught the stadium manager at the hockey arena rigging the goals."

Don, exhausted from the trip and still on an emotional high, didn't pay much attention to the scheme that Mark was describing. "The Hockey Goal is six-feet wide and four-feet high. Every period, the team changes goals and the two maintenance men come out and check the goal's measurements to insure standards.

"However, the maintenance men were expanding the width of the goal by six inches for the home team and shrinking the width of the goal by six inches on the visiting team. It definitely gave a huge advantage for the home team," he continued. "They did it by turning the top bar of the goal to enlarge or shrink it. There were small holes on the back of the top bar with small clamps that would hold the bar in place once slid into place to accommodate the compromised goal. A visiting fan filmed the act in progress and reported it to the press.

"Who would have ever guessed that the scheme would ever be noticed? "They charged the stadium manager with cheating and fined him ten thousand dollars and of course, he was fired! It was no coincidence that the home team won five games in a row! Think of the money that was won betting on the home team!

"Think about the shrinking or enlarging a basketball goal. Wow, what an advantage!"

Don was only partially listening to Mark. "Sure, Mark," he said, "let me know how that works out." Mark took the response as his dad's encouragement to explore the matter further. He was convinced that he could find a way. Mark suddenly envisioned himself as an anonymous hero for the Empire State basketball team. He could see the headlines in his mind: *Empire wins fifth straight home game!*

Don, suddenly interested, remembered that the new stand-alone basketball goals were scheduled to be delivered to Empire's gym the following day around 3:00 p.m. Don asked Mark if he can join him at the gym and take a close look at the new goals. Mark was enthusiastic at the prospects of being able to tip control the odds and immediately agreed to meet his father at the gym.

Lemmy, who was doing well at the guard position, was scheduled to play in the intersquad basketball game for Empire in a week or so. Don told Mark about the upcoming scrimmage and said he wanted Mark to attend with him. "I won't miss it," he said as he finished his meal, hugged Mark, and headed home to rest.

He was greeted warmly with a hug and a kiss from Karen. He slid into bed and it was only a matter of minutes before he was sound asleep and didn't awaken until around 5:30 p.m. – just in time for dinner. He stayed up only long enough to eat and watch the news before returning to bed for a long night's rest.

Chapter 22

THE FUN BEGINS

As he drove to the office Thursday morning, he hashed over in his mind everything that happened over the past several days. He began to analyze his potential financial gain. Attorney Jim Lewis was scheduled to meet with him at 11:00 a.m. in Don's office.

Still a little hung over and unable to wrap his brain around the whirlwind series of events just yet, he couldn't shake the thought that he was about to make more money than he ever imagined. being from a small town like Empire, it was all just too overwhelming. He decided to just keep his head down and let his attorney handle the details. He didn't want there to be any hidden surprises in the contracts so he wanted Jim Lewis to review them.

Greeting Matte, he retreated to his office. She brought him a cup of coffee and began stood by, awaiting her instructions to scheduling the day's activities. As he sat back in his comfortable chair, he couldn't help feeling a little smug.

He instructed Matte to call Dr. Roy Stevenson, the university president and invite him to join Don at 3:00 p.m. at the gym to look at the new goals that will be arriving. He was anticipating a full day of activity and was eager to get started. He called Vinney at the Sports bar just to make sure he would be there for lunch where he and Jim will have lunch.

"Of course, big man," Vinney said, "can't wait to hear about your trip."

Jim Lewis arrived right on time and Don didn't take long to summarize the events and the anticipated business he will be doing with MNS. Jim said that it would take him a day or two to review the agreements to see if everything was on the level and if he might see anything that Don should be aware of. Don quickly agreed and the two left for Vinney's and an early lunch.

Vinny greeted the pair at the door and walked them to a private table to the back of the sports bar where it was quieter. Vinney sat down with them as they ordered their food and drinks.

Don immediately informed Vinney that he was under a confidentiality agreement with the company that he would be working for and that he was unable to say much about anything except that he was extremely pleased.

"Don, I understand and I won't ask, I'm just happy for you!"

He told Vinney and Jim that he had an exhilarating experience at the casino in Atlantic City and that he understood how addictive gambling could be, especially when winning. His companions both laughed and Jim pointed out that it was fun to win but a "bitch" when you lose.

"Have you made your plays for the weekend?" Vinney asked, changing the subject.

Not wanting Jim to know that he was gambling, Don shrugged off the question, telling him instead about the sports book at the casino and it was really easy to bet on anything. Then, cryptically, he added, "No I could have, but I didn't."

Vinney caught his drift and deftly shifted the conversation to the upcoming basketball season at Empire University. Don reckoned that they should do pretty well because three seniors were returning for upcoming season. "In fact," he added, "At 3:00 p.m. today, they are delivering the new basketball goals that I'll be installing before the first game."

He explained about the new conference decision to unify all the arenas with goals will all have the red-light backboards synchronized to the shot clock and the game clock, thus eliminating any human error on last-second shots. Both his companions were that their gym will become first-class with the new goals.

Chapter 23

GOALS ARRIVE

Don arrived at the gym at 2:30 and met the maintenance supervisor, who introduced himself as Richard Lemoine. Together, they opened the huge garage door, through which large vehicles could enter to unload bulk items. The portal was also utilized for all other events that need special furniture or equipment. It's commonplace in all sports arenas to have an unloading area and pick up area such as this one.

Dr. Roy Stevenson arrived at precisely 3:00 p.m., just as the huge 18-wheeler rolled up to the delivery area where Don and the maintenance supervisor were standing. The 18-Wheeler did a half-circle and backed into the delivery area. The driver and three helpers exited the truck and Don introduced himself, Dr. Stevenson, and the Lemoine to the crew which would unload and install the new goal posts.

Mark has showed late but in time to witness the latest improvement to the gym. The helpers opened the back of the truck and the first item to be unloaded was a fork lift. There was a dock at the entrance, so the fork lift was able to easily roll out on an even plane with the back of the truck.

Like ants, the men assembling the goals moved quickly and efficiently and before long, both goal posts were erected and ready to apply the backboard The goals were made of clear, rectangular plexiglass and measured six-feet horizontally by three-and-a-half-feet vertically. The attached red lights were readily visible on the circumference of the back side of the backboard.

Mark noticed that the actual baskets would be last thing to be installed. As the helpers were taking a break, Mark asked his dad if he could take one of the baskets to the shop and study it. Don said he saw no problem but he reminded Mark that there was an intrasquad scrimmage a week from the following Thursday and the goals would have to be in place before then. He knew Mark was curious about how things work, so it wouldn't hurt to let him analyze the basket. At the same time, however, he wondered why.

Dr. Stevenson, Don and Richard Lemoine remain after the crew had left and admired the technology behind the new goals. Unlike the old goals which were lowered from the ceiling of the gym by a crank, these goals will be rolled in and out of place on a track that Don's men have installed as per the specs.

Once correctly positioned on the track, the wheels would be locked into place. The goals were supported by vertical support posts eighteen-by eighteen inches in width which were anchored inside a six-foot-by-six-foot base. The support posts stood ten feet high and a horizontal beam, the same size, connected to the vertical post support, much like a long arm cantilever hanging out over the baseline of the basketball court. It protruded four feet into the court and it provided the support to which the backboard was connected. The basketball goal was positioned precisely ten feet above the gym floor. Both beams were wrapped in soft foam cushions with Empire's blue and white school colors. The base was also covered in the same soft foam cushions to protect the players from getting injured during games, which can become quite physical despite the description of basketball as being a non-contact sport.

These goals put Empire University in the big leagues, Don thought, ignoring the fact that all schools were being required to equip basketball arenas similarly. Don had his electrician subcontractors install a floor outlet to connect electricity to the lights on the goal and to add a synchronizer to the shot and time clocks as well. They were scheduled to be finished in ample time for the scrimmage.

When Lemmy came home, he was equally effusive about the goals, saying that the whole team was so impressed with the new goals that they had a shoot-around that afternoon. He said that everyone asked where the other goal was and why it wasn't installed. Don kept his silence and didn't tell Lemmy that Mark took the goal to analyze it. Feeling that would only lead to unnecessary questions, Don told Lemmy that the crew setting up the goal, noticed a defect and took it back. It would be up shortly he assured his son. Lemmy, satisfied with the explanation and too disinterested to ask other questions, just nodded.

Chapter 24

DON'S BIG BET ON SUNDAY

Don has been so busy with MSN contracts, getting the new goals in place and taking care of normal business that he forgot he had a huge bet on the Bears +6.5 points on Sunday. His perspective on money had changed significantly since he is wheeling and dealing with several million dollars coming his way.

The next day, Friday, he called Matte and said he was taking the day off to rest and if anyone important calls, just forward him the message. After all, he told himself, he had done enough for one week. Also, it had been a most productive week.

Saturday, just to get out for a bit, he dropped by Vinney's for a sandwich and remembered as he walks into the sports bar that Vinney was not there. He was at the Saturday golf game at the club and Don told himself that he wouldn't be good anyway and besides, he needed to limit his stress. He headed home to watch some college football and then again, to take another bonus nap. Wow, what future earnings does to your psychic. Again, he counted on the $4.2 million from the MNS projects and the $1.2 million income from the renovation to the university gym. *Gosh, never thought a country boy from Niagara would become all this.*

Sunday morning Karen and Don attended the Sunday Service as always. After all, there may be something to all those prayers Don has been offering up. After church, Karen and Don headed to the grocery store to pick up some chicken to bar-b-que that night. Don's parents were invited but had to decline because of some prior engagement with one of the parishioners. When they arrived home Don anxiously turned on the Bears game. They were playing in New

York against the Giants. It was already the third quarter and not good! Giants 24, Bears 10. He still had a chance with the 6.5 points, just one score away. But not this day; final Giants 38, Bears 13. Don justified his loss to himself. *I have the $6,500 in the vault and if Golden comes by, I have it. After all, I won $1,000 the week before and $5,500 at the Casino. So, no problem, however, I need to listen to Vinney next time. Inside information is good stuff.* He grilled some chicken and with the boys that night they had a peaceful evening.

Don was feeling rested and sensed a new found energy. He was still excited about the future and couldn't wait to hook up with Vinney and catch up on the weekend. Once at the office, Don returned a few calls and then at 11:00 a.m., he arrived at Vinney's.

Vinney was smiling from ear to ear and Don could tell that he had something up his sleeve. "How was the golf game?" Don asked.

"My team won seventy-five big ones and boy did the other teams whine and whine. You should have been there!" Don shrugged and explained that he was just not up for the energy level that comes with that group. "I understand," Vinney said, "but listen do I have a hot one for tonight's game. It's Monday night football, baby."

Oh hell, can't wait to hear the spin on this one!

Vinney, not wasting a second, retreated to the private high-top table in the back corner of the bar. Don followed, thinking he could use a winner. They sat on the bar stools and Vinney, in a hushed voice, said, "Denver at home getting 3.5 against the Jets!"

"Okay, give me the scoop."

Grinning broadly, Vinney said in his best conspiratorial voice, said, "Denver at home enjoys the altitude that visiting teams do not. It's hard to adjust to that altitude in one day. Second, Denver is getting back their two Injured players: the all-pro linebacker and their star wide receiver. Third, the Jets are having locker room issues, they have lost three in a row and for the life of me, I cannot figure how the home team is getting points. Sure, they lost last week against the

Chiefs, but it was so cold, nobody could catch the ball. Denver missed a last-second 42-yard field goal to win by one. They're playing good ball and I'm going with them big time."

Don was taking all the information in. *Could it be this easy?*

Vinney continued to sell the "lock" but Don was already swallowing the spin hook, line and sinker.

Don quickly finished his lunch as he had a ton of work to get done. He realized that the gambling thing was taking too much of his time and his mind. As he arrived at the office, three sets of architectural drawings had arrived from MNS for his review. He also returned a call from Sally. "Good afternoon, Sally."

"Hello Don, I am just wondering how you're doing on reviewing the contracts?"

"I've got my attorney looking at them and he should be done in a couple of days. I'll call you as soon as he's finished.

Sally told Don not to worry but cautioned that they needed to complete that part of the equation in order to move forward with the projects.

"I understand," he said. "I'll call you by Wednesday."

I need to call Jim and get his comments immediately. He asked Matte to share the information with Jim and set up a meeting by Wednesday. He packed his briefcase and prepared to head home. He took advantage of the quite time to organize his business in his head.

Before leaving the office, he called Golden and bet Denver. The line was now Denver +3, it's dropped from +3.5. Don made the bet anyway for $5,500 to win $5,000. After all, Vinney has been on point so far. Don knew he was already down $5,500 and a loss tonight would put him down $11,000! He felt confident about the bet and believed everything was going his way now.

73. That night, the boys came over for dinner. Mark told his dad that the goal was back up and was in great working order. He asked

if he could wear a Williams Construction work shirt for the Thursday scrimmage. He said he would like to be able to test the shot clock with the scorer's table and look somewhat official. Don agreed and felt that it would appear that his company was on top of the installation – and operation – of the goals and the operation of the shot clock. Meanwhile, Lemmy was so excited about the upcoming scrimmage and he informed the family that he would be starting point guard on the White Team. Everyone said how great that would be and Lemmy would be able to show his skills to the head coach.

Karen, Don and Mark assured Lemmy they would be there to root him on and wish him all the success. Lemmy reminded them that the scrimmage would start at 5:00 p.m. Everyone was excited about the event and Lemmy just couldn't stop smiling.

After dinner, Don and Mark headed out to the patio to enjoy the sunset. Lemmy headed back to a night class. Overall, Don felt everything was going in the right direction. Don did not watch the Monday night game and went to bed early. Next morning, he read where Denver lost 21-10! Wow! A loss and $11,000 in the hole. *Well, there'll be other bets.*

Don met with Jim on Wednesday to go over the agreements with MNS. Jim told Don that he would have to carry OSHA insurance. Because his job as construction manager, he oversaw the methods of construction by the subcontractors and with that came the responsibility to keep the job safe. Don immediately called his agent, Pat Hight, to ask what the cost would be. He was told that it is approximately four percent of the total construction cost. Therefore, a $20 million dollar job would run around $80,000. Don indicated that he felt that was fair and that he'd get back to him when all the contracts were signed.

Otherwise, Jim said, everything has been reviewed and he recommended signing the agreements. Don was happy and called Sally to tell her the agreements would be sent by Fed Ex the following morning.

Chapter 25

THURSDAY SCRIMMAGE

Don arrived at the office around 9:00 a.m. and began his day by checking his emails. He Grabbed his usual cup of coffee as Matte informed him that Sally O'Brian had called. Don guessed that she received the agreements.

He called her and as soon as he heard her voice, he said, "Good morning, Sally, did you get the agreements?"

"Not yet, probably around ten this morning. But that's not why I called. I need to buy you breakfast next Tuesday or Wednesday, you available?"

"I should be, where?"

"I thought I'd make it easy for both of us. On I-120, exit 46 there is a place called the Sunrise House. It's about forty miles from me and about thirty miles from you. Say 9:30 a.m.?"

"I can do Tuesday next week," Don said. "Is that good?"

"Perfect." She asked a curious. "Don, how is your betting with Golden going?"

Don paused, wondering why she would be asking about his betting. "Well, Sally, up and down but I'm holding my own!"

"Good." See you next Tuesday."

Don hung up the phone and began to wonder if there something going on with Golden that he didn't. *Maybe she's worried about my gambling and doesn't want me to get too deep in the hole.*

Don has an otherwise uneventful day and arrived home at 4:00 p.m. to pick up Karen and head to the scrimmage. He wanted to get there a little early and watch the warmups. Karen said that Mark will meet them at the scrimmage. He had gone by the office to pick up his

Williams' work shirt and cap. Don was proud of Mark's participation and interest. It would show the crowd and the school administration that Don's company was on top of things.

When they arrived at the gym around 4:30, the teams were already warming up. There were seven players on each team, meaning that everyone would play in the scrimmage. The teams were wearing the team's jerseys with one team clad in light blue with white trim and the other team in white with blue trim. Lemmy was on the white team.

Mark was already there and wearing the Williams' work shirt which is evergreen in color with gold letters on the back proclaiming "Williams Construction Company." He was wearing a gold baseball cap with WCC written in evergreen on the front of the cap. He looks quite professional – a good look for the company, Don thought.

Mark was down on the court next to the goal posts checking on the electrical connections and watching the teams warm up. He walked over to the scorer's table and checked with the clock operator to ensure the shot clock is synchronized with the lights on the backboard. Everything was working perfectly and Mark finally satisfied, climbed the bleachers to join his parents. They were sitting ten rows up on the south side of the gym near the south goal. Across the court to their left was the north goal. A team's first half goal was determined by where the team's bench was located. Lemmy's team, the white team, was nearest the South goal. Accordingly, his team would be shooting the north goal in the first half. The blue team would be shooting at the South goal which was directly in front of the three. As Mark sats down, Don asked, "everything working?"

"Like a well-oiled machine," Mark replied.

At that moment the head coach, Al Armstrong, took the microphone and walked to center court. He welcomed everyone and proceeded to introduce the players on each team. The school band was cranked up and played a few fanfare notes as each player was introduced, creating the perfect background to get the teams and players pumped up. Then, Mark got up and walked back down to the south goal. He walked under the basketball rim, glanced at his phone and then for a few moments, looked up at the net hanging above.

Don guessed that there were about two hundred fans in attendance, a nice crowd for a scrimmage. Applause followed the playing of the National Anthem and the teams gathered center court for the start of the game. Senior "Big Ben" was the six-foot, eight-inch center for the blue team and Freshman Tim Devlin, who stood six-foot-six inches, was the center for Lemmy's white team.

The jump ball was won by the blue team and they quickly brought the ball toward the south goal. The ball was swung out to the forward on the wing and he shot for a three-pointer. The ball hits the rim and bounces out. The white team rebounded. Lemmy has already raced down to the north goal and a long pass is delivered to him and he makes an uncontested layup. Two-zip white team!

Don noticed that Mark had brought a yellow pad and was recording the attempted shots and the made shots. It quickly appeared that the white team was hot and the blue team was having trouble getting its shots to go in. At the half-way point of the first half, the white team led, 18-4. Lemmy had scored six points and looked confident and poised. The assistant coach for the blue team was not happy and was having a heated conversation with his team. After the time-out, game resumed with Big Ben received the ball under the goal and immediately went up for a slam dunk! "Boink, Clang," the ball refused to go down into the net. It appears that he did not slam it in the center of the goal. The white team got the rebound and again Lemmy was wide open downcourt for an easy layup! As the first half ended, the blue team was embarrassed to find itself on the short end of a lopsided 32-8 score. Lemmy was the leading scorer with 14 points. He'd made six shots, including one three-pointer and a free throw. He looked great and appeared to be catching the attention of the head coach.

During intermission, Mark went back down to the south goal, checked the electrical connections and again stood under the net looking at his phone and then up at the net. When he returned to his seat next to Don, Don asked, “is there something wrong with the goals?”

“Nope, the blue team just isn’t hitting their shots, that’s all!”

The white team got the ball first in the second half and began working the ball to the south goal. A quick shot from beyond the three-point line clanged off the goal. The blue team rebounded and immediately hit on a 12-foot jumper. “Finally!” the blue team assistant coach shouted as everyone in the gym applauded.

The white team was experiencing the same difficulty scoring on the south goal. They missed on all eight of their shots to open the second half and the blue team had scored fourteen points and had pulled to within ten points. The white team still led, 32-22, but by the ten-minute break in the half, the blue team had cut the white team’s lead to a razor-thin 35-31. Mark again headed down to the south goal and repeated his earlier routine of checking the electrical connections and standing under the goal for a minute looking as his phone and looking up at the net.

Don wondered but said nothing as Mark returned to his seat and grabbed his yellow pad to keep tracking the game. As the game continued, Lemmy hits a three-pointer from the top of the key, Karen and Don jump up applauding and shouting encouragement.

The game went back and forth and with a minute left, white team held a four-point lead. The blue team pulled to within one on a three-pointer. With twenty seconds to go, the white team had the ball and the freshman center was fouled, giving him a one-and-one free throw opportunity. If he makes the first one, he would get a second one. His first free throw hit the backboard and bounced into the hands of Lemmie who was immediately fouled. Ten seconds left and another one-and-one. Lemmie buried both free throws and the White Team led by three. The blue team hurried downcourt and heaved a long range three-pointer, which was nowhere close. The final score was white team 49, blue team 46.

Don, Karen and Mark made their way down to the court to congratulate Lemmy who was sweating profusely but smiling from ear to ear. Mark grabbed Lemmy and gave him a huge bear hug. It was almost as if Mark thought he won the game himself. Mark said that he would head home for a refreshment and see everyone there.

Chapter 26

WHAT THE HELL WAS THAT ABOUT?

When they arrived home, Mark was already sitting on the back porch, laughing as he sat in a rocking chair and sipped a beer. As Don walked out onto the patio with his beer, Mark stands up and walks over to exchange high-fives. Don, surprised at the burst of emotion, asked, “What the hell was that about?”

Without replying, Mark walked to the edge of the back porch and raised his arms like Sylvester Stallone in *Rocky* and yelled, “Damn right! I did it, I did it!”

Confused, Don asked, “What’re you talking about?”

Mark pulls his rocker up next to Don and looks him straight in the eye. “Dad, I did it, we’re on easy street at the Empire University basketball gym.” He got up and pulled the sliding door shut so his mom wouldn’t be able to hear his conversation with his dad.

“Dad, winning basketball is about one team getting the ball in the net more than the other team, am I correct?”

“Wow, what a revelation! So, what’s your point?”

“Well, the team that won tonight did just that! Got more balls in the net then the other team, you agree?”

“What the hell did you do?”

“Simple. Winning basketball is all about *nothing but net!* The team that drains the net the most wins!”

“What the hell did you do?” Mark repeated, more than a little curious by now.

“How many points were scored on the south goal in the first half?” Mark asked and without giving Don a chance to respond, said, his voice rising, “It was eight! “How many points were scored on the south goal in the first ten minutes of the second half? Three, just three! “How many points were scored in the final ten minutes of the game on the south goal? It was fourteen!”

“What were you doing looking at your phone under the south goal and then looking up at the goal? Don demanded. “What was that about?”

Mark paused, took a deep breath and then looked his dad straight in the eyes and said in a conspiratorial tone, “I rigged the south goal! I rigged the south goal!”

Don laughed in spite of his shock and incredulity and said, “You’re delusional, you must be on drugs!”

“Okay, I’ll let you know how I did it.” But just as Mark was about to explain his secret to Don, Lemmy burst through the door, feeling like a hero.

“How did I do?” he asked, already knowing the answer, but wanting confirmation from those closest to him. The entire family accommodated him, praising his performance in the scrimmage.”

“Was it just me, or did it seem that there was something wrong with the south goal?

Mark laughed nervously, and joked, “The floor must be uneven on that end of the gym. What else could it be? Maybe it’s just bad shooting.”

They all go in to share pizza and just enjoy a good night as a family. As Don headed off to bed, he told Mark to meet him for lunch at 11:00 a.m. the following day at Vinney’.!

FRIDAY LUNCH, THE EXPLANATION

Don arose early Friday anticipating the lunch with Mark and his explanation of "rigging the goal." After rehashing the scrimmage in his mind, he sensed there was something odd about the south goal after all, but how does one "rig a goal?" He arrived at the office around 8:30 a.m. and Matte, as usual, had already made the coffee and had a list of appointments for the following week. As he read over the list of things to do, he reminded himself of the "lock" Vinney had for him the coming Monday night. He decided he would ask him to repeat his opinion on why it was a good play.

As he did so, he saw the upcoming appointment with Sally and wondered again, why she wanted to know how he was doing with Golden. He shook his head, pushed his appointment book away, and moved on to the business of the day. He took his coffee into the conference room where his estimator was pouring through the three sets of architectural drawings that Don's company would participate in as construction manager. The task was for Don's company to do its own estimating and see how close it was to the MSN development company's anticipated budget. After all, Williams Construction company would be responsible for bringing the projects close to the estimated budget.

Don left for Vinney's and grabbed the customary private high-top in the back of the bar. Vinney waved at Don and said, "I'll see you after a while, I'm busy right now."

That was fine for Don as he and Mark would need some private time anyway. Mark entered holding his yellow pad and grinning broadly.

"Okay, wise guy, tell me what the hell happen!"

Mark, deliberately dragging out the suspense for all the drama he could milk out of the moment, waved to the waitress to take his order. When she left, Mark leaned toward Don and, in almost a whisper, said, "Okay, Dad, this is very confidential and very exciting."

“Let me have it,” Don said impatiently. “What the heck were you doing staring up at the basketball rim and then looking down at your phone?”

“Dad, do you know the diameter of a basketball goal is eighteen inches?”

“Well, to tell the truth, I never really thought about it.”

Mark, paying no attention to Don’s answer, continued, “Do you know that you can fit two regulation basketballs inside the rim at the same time, because they are both nine Inches in diameter? So, what if you could somehow change the diameter of the goal to assist one team and change the diameter to hurt the other team? Remember when I took the goal with me last week? Well, I wanted to look at a way mechanically, that I could enlarge and shrink the goals by utilizing the interior of the orange connector that ties the rim to the backboard.

“What?” Don asks, a shocked expression suddenly exploding across his face.

“What I did was splice the rim inside the connector and add two small steel cylinders that connect the rim on each side. The cylinders are connected and rotate the rim inside the connector, like an electric drill. There are two small motors that work in unison to propel the cylinders. Both cylinders operate in sync and push or pull the rim depending on whether I want to shrink the rim or increase it.

“The standard goal has a diameter of eighteen inches. By pulling the rim inside the connector by approximately six inches, I can decrease the diameter by three inches, making the diameter of the rim fifteen inches. That is what I did to the south goal last night. I left the north goal at eighteen inches all night just to see what would happen. I also increased the width of the connector from eight inches to twelve inches giving the needed room on the inside of the connector to expand and contract the rim to affect the diameter!”

Don was incredulous at what he is hearing and was rendered speechless as Mark continue: “I also hollowed out the first 6 inches of the rim on both sides and created threads inside the rim that the push and pull would come from the drill motion. Last, I cut small slices on the exterior of the rim itself creating a more flexible rim to expand and decrease with the desired diameter. The tensile strength is not compromised by the slices in the rim, since the slices are cut to a minimum depth. I then put all the pieces back together, painted the entire structure original orange."

"What were you doing under the goal with your phone?" Don demanded.

"This is the coolest part! I have the motors hooked up to Bluetooth on my phone. So, Dad, we can sit on the first bleacher on the court and activate each goal without getting closer. I was just looking up to see the goal shrinking. Think about it. No one will ever suspect what's going on. It does take forty-five seconds to complete the desired task. So, if they stop the game to check the diameters, by the time they get the ladders to measure, I'll have the diameter back to the standard 18 inches."

"Bluetooth, I don't know how that works."

"It's easy and no batteries and I can control it through an app in my phone. I added an additional electric connection to the connector to operate the small motors."

"You haven't taken down the north goal yet?"

"No sir, not yet, I'm going to do that this weekend." Mark replied.

Vinney at that moment approached. "What are you guys into, I see some heavy conversation?"

Without missing a beat, Mark asked, "Vinney we were just wondering if there will be a line on next week's Empire basketball game."

"I'm sure there will be. They're a Division One school."

"Well, I hope so," Don said.

Nothing more was said about Mark's creation. They had a quiet lunch and Don asked Mark to come by the house after work so they could finish their conversation about Mark's remarkable new invention at home.

Chapter 27

DON'S SPINNING HEAD

As Don drove back to the office, he found himself still trying to wrap his brain around what Mark just explained to him. He then let's out a loud laugh. *That son of mine, where did he come up with this? Yes, I saw the balls bounce off the rim on the south goal, no one seemed to be able to make a basket, I still don't believe it but I saw it with my own eyes. If this works like Mark thinks it will, then we can win every bet we make on Empire at home!* Then Don's inner soul reaches out to him and says, *"You are not a cheater."*

But greed quickly took over. *I'll have to start with little bets not to alarm Golden, he'll catch on real quick if I start winning big on Empire. The Vegas cats will certainly notice the edge Empire has at home games and will immediately adjust the line accordingly.*

Don checked out early and headed for some quiet meditation and more questions he wanted to ask Mark later that night. Once home, he relaxed in his big chair. A wave of calm and confidence hit him all at once and suddenly the world was perfect. The calming feeling led to him falling asleep.

Don awoke a couple hours later and learned that Mark was going out with the boys and would not be home that night. Don, a little disappointed knew hed catch up with Mark over the weekend.

Meanwhile, Lemmy came in and they have a nice family conversation around dinner. Karen made spaghetti and she and Don shared a glass of wine. Lemmy controled the conversation around the basketball team and the upcoming game against Northern Penn University. Lemmy said that Northern Pen was a really good team. They had an all-conference center who is seven-foot, two-inches tall and weighed three hundred twenty-pounds. His name was Maximo Gheato and he was from Romania. His nickname was "King Kong!"

"He averages twenty-four points and eighteen rebounds per game and no one can stop him," Lemmy said. "They won their conference with a record of twenty-two wins and just three losses and went to the second round of March Madness, losing to Villanova by six points."

Don asked about Empire's Center, Big Ben. Lemmy said, "He's six-foot, eight-inches and weighs about 260. "Dad he'll get waxed by 'King Kong.' He's projected to be a first-round pick in the NBA draft next year." Don stared at Lemmy without speaking as his mind went directly to thoughts of the wager he wanted to make on Empire for the following Saturday night. He now believed that the line will be at least fifteen points with Empire being a heavy underdog.

Don was thinking it would be fun to watch Mark's invention against a player of King Kong's caliber. *Oh well, I really don't have to bet the game, just be a fan and enjoy the game.*

THE WEEKEND

Saturday morning, Don again opted not to play golf and headed to his office to prepare for the coming week. He was still curious about why Sally asked about his betting with Golden. He decided she was probably just concerned about him and didn't want him to wrapped up too deeply in gambling with so much at stake on the upcoming projects. He didn't make any football bets for Saturday or Sunday but was beginning to change his mind about making a small bet on Empire basketball the following Saturday. That will be fun to watch. It turned out to be a quiet weekend until Mark came over after church on Sunday and informed his dad that "the north goal is all set!"

Don took the opportunity to ask Mark about the reliability of his invention. "Mark how sure are you that this Bluetooth thing will function the way you want it to?"

"Dad, I've spent the last three hours checking the functions and they are working perfectly. I can't wait to place a bet on the first game. Have you seen a line yet?"

"Won't be out till next Wednesday I am told," his dad replied.

"Well, I pity the poor team that plays us and the bookie or sports book that we bet with!"

Don said nothing, but thought how sweet that would be; a lock Doesn't happen every day in sports.

Don asked, "Do you know who we are playing Saturday?"

"Naw, it doesn't matter Dad, that team will get so frustrated that they will lose their cool. Empire will look a pro team on both defense and offense. Just imagine the advantage our boys will have."

Don attributed his optimism to youth exuberance and let his prediction pass, knowing his wager will be so small that it would still be a lot of fun to watch, no matter the outcome.

Mark added, "Dad, just so you know, I left both goals at eighteen-inch diameters so everything will be in order until next Saturday's game."

Monday

Monday morning at the office was quiet. Don returned calls and answered a few emails. He then headed over to Vinney's to check up on things. He would not comment on the Denver game since he now has what he believes is a sure thing – like shooting fish in a barrel. That is, if Mark's invention is reliable.

Vinney, in his usual upbeat mood, sat with Don and apologized about the latest bet on Denver. "Don, they never lose at home on Monday night and they always cover.

“Well, we’ll have to do better next time,” Don replied. He did let Vinney know that he is eleven thousand dollars in the hole to Golden and he hoped that Golden had not shared that bit of confidential information with Vinney. It wouldn’t be right for Vinney to know everything about Don’s bets. He thought about winning big on Empire’s first game but didn’t want to arouse any suspicion because it was critical that no one should know how he was doing it. It would lead to big trouble for the Williams family, if the truth were to be revealed.

Chapter 28

TUESDAY BREAKFAST WITH SALLY

Tuesday morning, Don headed over to the Sunrise House around 8:45 a.m. He figured he should arrive around 9:15am, just a little early and that is something that shows respect, being on time. As he drove, he again wondered what the meeting would be about. It gnawed at him and in his head, he reviewed his business with Sally. He knew he’d done every asked of him so far.

He allowed his mind to turn positive about all of the exciting things that were going to happen with his business, Lemmy’s basketball season, and a world of happy times ahead. He almost got chills thinking about his life ahead. *I’ve positioned myself so well that this is almost unbelievable.* He allowed himself to let self-pride creep into his feelings – pride for himself and pride for his family.

He turned up the music on his favorite radio station and found himself singing along with the music. It didn’t matter that he couldn’t carry a tune – no one could hear him anyway. He then laughed at himself as his thoughts again returned to the upward turn in his life and career.

The hostess greeted him at the door of the “Sunrise House and he requested a private booth, if possible. She seated him on the far end of the restaurant where it was quite and private. Perfect, he thought and he settled in to wait for Sally to arrive.

Right on time, Sally walked in at 9:30 a.m. and Don waved to her. Seeing him, she headed his way. She was dressed in a black jumpsuit with a navy blue scarf around her neck. *Wow! What a beautiful woman.*

As they met, they hugged and exchanged hellos. Anyone observing would be able to can tell that they are both happy to see each other. They both ordered coffee and breakfast and settled in for the purpose of the meeting, which remained a mystery to Don.

"Sally, everything good on your end?"

"Yes, let's just chit chat, then after we have breakfast, I'll fill you end on the latest."

Don, ever more curious by now, agreed. In an effort to make small talk, he asked if she had been back to the Casino. She said yes, but it wasn't as successful as when she went with Don.

"Well, I must have been your good luck charm."

She agreed and the conversation continued in that vein as they talked about the weather, sports and family. He told her about Lemmy and the upcoming basketball season and how excited he was about that. She agreed that it must be exciting to see one's son out on the court. Don continued to talk about all of the dynamics that come with a basketball game but the conversation somehow seemed forced, stilted, as each sensed the tension that had sneaked into their meeting.

They finished breakfast and order more coffee when Don, trying to force the subject of the meeting to the surface, said, "So, are we still on track with MNS Development?"

That brought an abrupt change in the mood. Sally hesitated for a moment that said more than she wished. Finally, she said, "Don, unfortunately, we have an issue that has come up and it's going to affect all of us!" Her tone suddenly serious and dark, she continued,

“We have a problem with Golden and a builder by the name of Sam Butler. What I am about to tell you is of course very, very confidential. MNS Development is an arm of HRVSL. That stands for Hudson River Valley Savings and Loan, as you know.

“MNS uses HRVSL loans to build the projects and also uses cash to pay for them. About thirty percent of the projects are paid in cash and the rest through a loan. The cash comes from the Casino and the Bookies. We have nine bookies in the northeast like Golden.

“So, let’s say a project costs $20 million to build, then around $6 million in cash is used to pay for labor and materials, which is the thirty percent. The subcontractors love it and the benefit for HRVSL is that they list the loan at 70% of that $20 million which is $14 million on the books. However, they get the project appraised once it is up and running for twenty million dollars plus. Then MNS Development Co. refinances the debt for the full twenty million and six million in washed through the books. That gives them a tax free additional six-million-dollar asset! Don, my bosses are washing money and making the Savings and Loan a huge profit. Yes, it’s absolutely illegal and between Sam Butler and Golden, they are about to bring the house down!”

“How well do you know Golden?” Don asked.

She looks at Don for several seconds, hesitant to speak. Finally, she said, “He’s my father. I barely remembered him until he tracked me down at the savings and loan. Of course, I’ve always been angry at him.

but once he explained what happened, I realized he did the best he could do at that time and I’ve achieved my success on my own. I helped him get his license in Newark through my bosses and it's worked out pretty well for him.

Don was stunned at what he was hearing and didn’t comment because he knew there was more and he wanted to hear the rest of the story.

She continued, "Sam and Golden know all about this money laundering because they're a part of it and that's the problem. Sam is on the books for about three million dollars because he was supposed to be reimbursed for invoices he signed for and it's almost 180 days in arrears. Golden is supposed to be reimbursed for losses to the tune of $300,000 and Dee Lombart refuses to reimburse him because he thinks he is rigging the books. The bookies all fax me their daily action and I double check their balances every Monday morning. They also send me their taped recorded bets and I erase the recorded bets for security reasons.

"On the first of the month, I check all the bookies wins and losses for the company before I submit the information to the savings and loan. A few months back, Golden sent in a bet made by Spanky for $300k and Golden reported that he paid Spanky. Spanky has no memory of the bet and says he never made the bet and he would have remembered being paid the $300k. Golden cannot produce his recorded bet and I have to agree with Mr. Lombart, Golden is trying to pull a fast one.

Golden he keeps everything on each bettor on a yellow pad in his office, all hand written. No computers, too easy to track. I've seen the yellow pad where you won a thousand dollars from him earlier. Once one is paid off or your losses are paid, Golden destroys the ledger with a paper shredder. I saw last week on your pad at Golden's office where he raised your gambling limit to $25,000 and as of last Monday night, you are down $11,000. That is why I asked you about your position with Golden.

The bookies have a great deal. They are paid twenty percent of their winnings and the company pays all of their losses. On average, our bookies win six hundred thousand a year and take home a hundred thousand or more.

"All of this shortfall is because of a couple of things. One, the pandemic kept people out of the casino and two, raising interest rates hurt the savings and loan because people quit borrowing money. We're shutting down projects at the moment and your projects have been put on the back burner. I'm sorry Don, and to make matters worse, there is a county commissioner who was selling building permits for five thousand dollars each and one of the builders in that county reported him to the FBI.

"He was approached by the FBI and they cut a deal with him for a lighter sentence if he would wire up and try to catch other builders. Well, guess who they hooked? Sam Butler, one of our builders. He was caught on camera handing the commissioner five grand in cash to get his building permit.

"So now, Sam is screwed unless he can help the government bring in more perps. His ace in the hole of course is MNS Development and DLSL and those are monster catches for the Government. Sam being owed three million is in no mood to play around anymore. He's contacted me and explained his position. I'm sitting on the information for now and working on a strategy to get everyone out of this horrible position we're in right now."

As Don's mind was spinning, she continued, "Don, you will be okay, but you have to clear your debt to Golden by winning a bet! Otherwise, he will eventually rat on you and you will become a co-conspirator in huge money laundering case. He's my dad, but he'll bring the whole house of cards down, just to save himself! Your reputation and your life as you know them will be over. I'm putting you on high alert here. This is as serious as a heart attack. The shit is about to hit the fan! My dad's a rat and I've lost all respect for him. So please, Don, clear your debt or you will go to jail for a long time!"

Don, who had listened in rapt attention without speaking, took a deep breath and finally spoke. "Sally I'm sick to my stomach. I don't want to come down on your bosses and I'm grateful that you came to me and you want to protect me." Unable to express his feelings further, he simply stopped talking, head in a deep, dark cloud.

"I am sorry Don. Things happen around us that we cannot control. I have to go but you let me know up the minute on your dealings with Golden."

"I will Sally," he replied in a barely audible whisper.

He walked her to her car where they exchanged a brief hug.

In his car, Don just sat and stared at the dashboard. At that moment, a rage of anger came over him, causing him to uncharacteristically lose control of his emotions and he pounded on the steering wheel, screaming, "MoFo, mofo, mofo!!" as he did so.

Chapter 29

COOLER MINDS MUST PREVAIL

As Don pulled onto the Interstate back to Empire, he called Matte in a sense of urgency he managed to conceal and told her to call Mark and tell him to meet him at Deano's for lunch at 11:30 a.m. The most important thing to do now was to win eleven thousand dollars from Golden and clear his name off the board, to wipe out his debt before the feds raided his office. For now, Mark's little invention could be the ticket to freedom. He knew he would have to bet $12,100 to cover the ten percent fee and to win eleven thousand. There couldn't be any hesitation at this point, it was like jumping out of an airplane and hoping the parachute worked.

Don checked in with Karen and let her know he would come home after his lunch with Mark. By the tone of his voice, she realized things didn't go well. Wives are like that but she learned long ago not to ask any direct questions. He would let her know the outcome of the meeting in good time. Knowing him the way she did, she cautioned him not to drink too much at lunch. He promised her he wouldn't but said he would have a least one drink.

As Don walked into Deano's, he headed straight to the bar. He told Billy the bartender to make him a very dry martini, chilled and shaken with one olive. The drive had been longer than expected, so he headed to the restroom. When he returned to the bar, Billy said for him to sit wherever he would like. There were several booths and he found the one at the end of the bar that offered the most privacy.

Don asked Billy what kind of soup was on the menu when told it was French onion, he told Billy, "I'm waiting on my son, so I'll have the soup when I order.

Mark arrived right on time and joined Don at the booth. He saw that his dad had just finished one martini and had ordered a second. "Dad, you ok? Have you had a bad morning?"

Before Don answered, he took a big drink of the second martini and looked directly at Mark. "Well, son, I think I've got a dirty bookie and he's making some trouble for me and will bring me down with him unless…"

He stopped there, realizing that he must be very careful how much he explains to Mark. So, he pivoted and said, "It seems he is very careless and he isn't private with people's business. He's proud to let other people know of your downfall and weaknesses. It makes him look good and that's what he wants.

"You know your grandpa doesn't condone gambling and if word got out that I'm gambling and has dug myself a hole, well it would be so embarrassing for him and my mother – not to mention the gossip that would quickly spread all over this town."

Mark, not exactly naïve, instantly saw that his dad was crying out for help.

"Dad, I don't care how big a hole you've dug, by damn, we can beat this no-good sonofabitch Saturday by betting on Empire. In fact, I've gotten the line and we are twelve-and-half-point underdogs to Northern Penn. Dad, I am confident with the goals being manipulated our way, it's a lock. I've just come from the gym and both goals are working perfectly. Why don't you take the rest of the day off and tomorrow around 11:00 a.m., we can meet at the gym and I'll show you how the system works."

Don, feeling both despondent and slightly drunk, agrees, telling Mark he would love that. He quickly finished his soup and headed home to try to forget about his morning.

Don took the back roads home, driving slowly for safety and once he arrived, he immediately retreated to the bedroom. Karen said she'd awake him around 4:00 p.m. He was asleep immediately. When he awoke, the conversation with Sally kept haunting him. *Hell, I can't escape this nightmare!* He walked over to the vanity and washed his face and tried to feel revived. *Tomorrow, I will be proactive*.

Chapter 30

WEDNESDAY, A DAY OF NEW INFORMATION

He awoke around 7:00 a.m. from a restless night of fitful sleep. He knew he shouldn't drink at lunch and he was now angry at himself for letting his emotions make decisions for him. He dressed quickly and headed out to the office to meet his newest challenges. Karen handed him a cup of coffee to go and wished him a nice day. At least he could still feel grateful that he had a wife who is very well-grounded and gave me all of the love and support one man could ever want.

Getting to the office early and sitting at his desk provided a feeling of serenity and a sense of organization for his demeanor that he really needed at this time. The first thing he needed to find out was if Golden would take a bet on the Empire game. There was no reason to think otherwise, but if he says he won't, then Don felt he'd be screwed. *If he does, then Mark's contraption has to work and we need to win the bet!* He realized that there was nothing he could do to help himself except to clear his books with Golden. Again, his conscience spoke to him, *you are not a cheater!*

Mark then wrote down all of his future income possibilities and shook his head at the stark realization that the potential $4.2 million income from the MNS Development was not going to happen. He still couldn't believe what Sally had told him. Don knew she wouldn't lie to him about something this monumental. He wondered what the end result would be for the development company and the savings and loan and he thought about what a massive hit it would be on so many people. Looking at his check list, he knew that settling his affairs with Golden was paramount to his future!

Time has a way of getting away and before he realized it, it was 8:30 and Matte walked in. "Surprised to see you here," she said.

"Yeah, I needed to get started early on a couple of things."

Matte made coffee and brought him a fresh cup.

Thanking her, he asked her if anything pressing was on the day's calendar and said no, he had all his bases covered for the day.

"Great. I'll be out this morning from 10:30. I'll be back after lunch.

He planned to meet with Mark and the two of them would drop by Vinny's after the gym demonstration and grab lunch. Don, in trying not to be too obvious or too aggressive with Golden, would ask Vinney to call Golden and see if he was taking bets on basketball and specifically, Empire for Saturday Night.

THE DEMONSTRATAION

Don arrived at the gym at 11:00 and found Mark already there. In fact, Mark had already brought out the twelve-foot ladder for his dad to get a close-up look at the movement of the rim.

"What is it you want me to do here?"

"First, Dad, we are going to use this tape measure and check the height of the rim from the floor. Just climb up there and hold the tape on the rim and hand me the tape measure and I'll place it on the floor. He did, and Mark said that it was exactly ten feet – regulation height.

Mark then handed the tape measure back to Don and said, "Now stretch the tape across the diameter of the rim." Don did as he was instructed and said it was eighteen inches exactly

"Okay, you ready? Keep the tape stretched across the rim and watch what happens." Don looked down and could see Mark playing with his phone. He was watching the rim when suddenly, it started to shrink from eighteen inches to seventeen. Slowly, it moved to sixteen inches and finally, to fifteen inches, where it stopped.

"What you got up there?"

"I've got 15 inches!" came the flabbergasted reply.

"Good! Keep watching." In about half a minute, Don sees the rim enlarging back to sixteen inches, then to seventeen and then to eighteen inches.

"The rim is back to its original diameter," Don yells, a little too loudly. Fortunately, there was no one in the gym to hear them. As he watched, the rim kept enlarging to nineteen inches, then to twenty and finally, twenty-one 21 inches.

What's it look like now? Mark asked.

Don, astounded, said, "I don't believe it, it's twenty-one inches in diameter!" He was grinning from ear to ear as he climbed down the ladder. Once on the floor, he grabbed Mark and in a bear hug that nearly took Mark's breath. "You son of a gun, you did it, you little bastard!" He was jumping up and down with Mark like they'd just won the Super Bowl

Don backed away finally and asked, "The other goal works too?"

"Absolutely" Mark said, laughing aloud. Suddenly, silence fell over the gym as each pondered the potential impact of what they had. One could hear a pin drop in the dead silence as the reality of what they had sank in. Mark grabbed the ladder and headed to the store room with it as Don, now laser focused, told Mark to meet him at Vinney's. There they would learn if they would be able to place a wager with Golden on the upcoming Empire game.

Chapter 31

NERVOUS MOMENTS

As he drove to Vinney's, Don convinced himself that Golden would take a bet on Empire. After, all they were playing a defending conference champion and giving 12.5 points to Empire seemed a safe bet on paper. But as they say, the game isn't played on paper. As Don walked into Vinney's, he headed to his usual high-top table way in the back. Mark arrived shortly and found Vinney and Don talking.

"Vinney," Don asked, "do you think Golden will book the Empire basketball game this Saturday?"

Vinney did not respond but instead, immediately called Golden on his cell phone. The moment represented a turning point in Don's life and was upset with Vinney taking it so lightly. *What if Golden says no?* "Hello, Golden," Vinney said, "I got a man here wants to know if you will accept a basketball bet on Empire this Saturday?" A couple of seconds later, Vinney, laughing, said to Don. "Golden wants to know what you know about basketball, he says you can't even win a football bet!"

Don's emotions had been on a roller coaster the whole week and now he had to confront Golden to place on bet on the Empire game. Don grabbed the phone from Vinney and tells him he needed his office. "Hold on, Golden," he said, "I need some privacy." Don walks into Vinney's office behind the bar and closed the door, took a deep breath as he sat in Vinney's office chair.

"Well, Golden, you got me down and I'm looking for a way out. I want to bet the Empire game this Saturday and I want you to book it."

Don could hear Golden chuckling. "well it looks like I've got a wild horse on my hands and Don, I love wild horses!"

"Well, you going to book it or not?"

“Hold on cowboy, let me see if there is a Vegas line on the game.

He could hear Golden typing on his computer, looking for Saturday’s basketball odds.

“Yep,” he finally said. “Penn’s a twelve-and-a-half-point favorite, let me keep reading. Shit Don, Penn has an NBA prospect in this Center. Hell, he is seven-foot, two-inches tall and weighs in at three-twenty. Was all conference last year averaging twenty-four points a game and eighteen rebounds. Don, I won’t book your bet because you’ll lose this game and the bet.”

“You chicken shit,” Don spat, “I want to bet this game!”

“Okay, it’s your funeral,” Golden said. “How much you want to bet?”

Don asks, “How much do I have to bet to wipe out my eleven-thousand debt to you?”

“Whoa Cowboy, you’ve got some brass balls. Let’s see, ten percent added to eleven grand is $12,100. You have to bet $12,100 to break even.”

“I want to bet $12,100 and I want you to record you confirming my bet!”

“Good thing you got some big jobs coming because you’re going to need the dough if you keep making bad bets. Okay, I am booking Don Williams for $12,100 to win eleven thousand dollars on the Empire vs Northern Penn basketball game, this Saturday, Dec. 11th. Empire will be getting 12.5 points as the underdog.” “Okay, Don, I’m playing it back to you now.” Don heard the recording and took a deep breath and said to Golden, “Thank you and goodbye!”

Don returned to the table where Vinney and Mark were talking. Don handed the phone back to Vinney and thanked him.

“Did he take your bet?”

Don nodded. “I called him a chicken shit and I think it got him mad and yes, I am down for the game this Saturday. Vinney looked at both Don and Mark and asked, "Is there something I'm missing about this game? You guys are so damned determined to bet on Empire. Is there something funny going on?"

Mark couldn't hold back. He laughed and said, "Well, Mr. Vinney, we just believe in Lemmy!"

Vinney shook his head and said, "Well, I'll take a look at the game, but from where I sit, Empire should be getting twenty points, not twelve-and-a-half."

Don was mentally exhausted from the last twenty minutes he had spent in dealing with getting his bet booked and hopefully his life back on track. He headed back to his office, feeling relieved that he got a bet down to wipe out his debt and sleep good at night again.

Chapter 32

THURSDAY, FRIDAY

On Thursday morning Don arrived at his office around 9:00. He sat down in his chair, ready to start the day. Matte came in to tell him that the architect, Bill King, had called and would like to set an appointment the following Thursday at 10:00 a.m. to review his preliminary plans on the renovation of the Empire State gym. He said he saw no problem and told Matte to get Joe, the estimator, on the line. I want to make sure he's available that day. Then Matte told Don that Sally O'Brian has called and she would like a call back.

Don said he would call her back but wanted to talk to Joe first. "Good morning, Joe, how are you doing?" Don said when Joe answered.

"I'm good Mr. Don, how are you?"

"I'm good. I need to find out if you're available next Thursday at 10:00 a.m. I've got the architect coming here to review his preliminary plans for the renovation of the Empire State Gym. We can begin to estimate the project after we see his plan and specifications."

"Yes sir, I'll be there."

"Great and also Joe, I need you to come by the office and get our camera. I want you to go out to the gym and take pictures of both the inside and outside. Get them developed into eight-by-ten color photos for us to have while we discuss the plans."

"Yes sir, I'll get it done, see you next Thursday," Joe says.

Don asked Matte to confirm the meeting with architect Bill King and to get Sally on the phone. Moments later, Matte said, "She is on."

"Good morning, Ms. O'Brian, how are you doing?"

Without exchanging greetings, Sally came right to the point: "Well, when you make a 'must bet,' you throw caution to the wind! Hell Don, you've got a David vs. Goliath situation going here.

"Oh, I almost forgot, you got the fax from Golden this morning on my bet on Empire this Saturday Night, didn't you?"

"Yes, I did! Don, do you think Empire can even stay on the court with this NBA prospect? I also see that they have two other returning starters and they won their conference easily last year." She sounded worried. "You bet $12,100!"

"Hell, Sally, I have got to get out of the hole now! Besides, I feel good about getting 12.5 points on our home court. And like you said last week, I have to clear the books with Golden or else."

"Don, you're a big boy and I just pray for your sake that this'll all work out."

"Thanks, Sally, I know you're on my side. Do you have any updated news on this secret investigation?"

"No, but that doesn't mean they're not moving into position to take all of us down. We don't know what Sam is telling them or whether they've contacted Golden yet. So, Don, your job right now is to win that bet Saturday Night. I have to go Don, got a lot of work to do and I'll be praying for you on Saturday."

As soon as they hang up, Mark called." Good morning son, what's going on?"

"Dad the Vegas line has moved to Northern Penn giving Empire 15.5 points. There's some smart money moving out there and they don't believe in Empire."

Don looked up at the ceiling. *Bring it on Lord, things are getting a little spooky now, I need you to pull me through this one*. "Mark," he said without hesitating, "today I want you to write down a list of things that could go wrong with your invention Saturday night. Come by the house for supper. We need to prepare for the unknown and to be able to fix them on the spot!"

Mark, sensing some panic in his dad's voice, replied, "Sure, Dad. I'll work on that and I'll see you around 5:30 tonight."

Don sat back in his chair and started to take deep breaths, trying to keep from hyperventilating. He wasn't prone to panic attacks but the emotion was building. It was like a freight train coming right at him and the only thing to stop it from running over him were two small motors inside a couple of basketball goals. Those were his only defenses! *What a mess I'm in!* He shut his eyes and suddenly, the nightmare of arrested began to sink in. *Holy shit*. He shook his head, and dared to open his eyes only to realize how close he was to handcuffs.

He looked at the clock and it was 10:30 a.m. He got up and started to walk out door. As he did so, Matte asked where was going. "I'm going to the club to hit some balls and have some lunch. I'm going home after that. I'll be taking a day off tomorrow and I want you to do the same. Just forward the incoming calls to your cell phone. I don't expect anything of consequence will happen tomorrow because we're not here." He then peeled two one-hundred-dollar bills out of his pocket and placed them on her desk. "I want you to have a good weekend and I just want you to know that I appreciate all of your loyalty and hard work."

In his car, Don called Vinney and invited him to hit balls with him at the range and to have lunch afterward. But Vinney said that he has a busload of tourists coming in for lunch headed to the Falls and that he had to stay and work to take care of them. Don said would see him Saturday morning at the club. He then called the caddie master, Sal, to have him place his clubs and shoes on a cart for him so that they'd be ready when he got there.

Upon arriving at the club, he found his clubs and shoes on a golf cart ready to roll. He handed Sal a ten and thanked him for setting everything up. He drove the golf cart to the driving range and proceeded to hit a few balls with every club before heading to the chipping and putting green, where he spent about thirty minutes getting comfortable with his stroke. Once he finished practicing, he headed into the Grill Room where he found a couple of his friends who played golf on Saturday. He sat with them, enjoying light conversation for a while before heading home to shower and just unwind.

Once home, he showered, put on a sweat suit and climbed into bed. He felt like just licking his wounds and sleep.

Around 5:00, Karen entered the bedroom. "Time to wake up or you won't be able to get to sleep tonight."

Don sits up and hugs her and she said they are having short ribs and mashed potatoes for dinner but that he might first like to join her in a glass of wine.

Red wine is awaiting him by his lounge chair in the family room. They sat quietly, enjoying their wine.

At that time, Mark walked in and seeing his parents in something of a private moment together, asked, "Am I disturbing something?" They laugh and Don told Mark they were just enjoying each other's company. Mark walked into the kitchen and opened a bottle of beer and sat down joined them. He asks if Lemmy was coming for dinner and Karen said he'd be running a little late but would be home. "Great," Mark said, "I want an update on his team's mental state for Saturday night."

"Yes, that will be nice to hear," Don said, "but let's not put pressure on him, he's got a lot on is plate, for sure!"

"I agree Dad. I also have the construction suggestions that I've gathered concerning the renovation of the new gym," Mark said, attempting to be coy in front of his mother.

"Of course," Don says. "We'll get some fresh air and you can tell me about it in a few minutes."

Karen sensing a father-son business discussion, told them she was going to continue to get dinner ready and she headed to the Kitchen. Don got up and headed to the patio to hear about the "Unknowns!"

Once outside on the patio, they both sat facing each other. Mark pulled out a sheet of paper and said, "Number one, electricity is our friend. If the power goes out, I'll have to reboot the Bluetooth inside the connector when the power comes back on. I've spoken to Mr. Lemoine, the maintenance supervisor already. There's an old but working Generator out back by the gym. It's a natural gas generator. However, you have to manually flip the switch to utilize the natural gas to fire it up. Back when it was installed, the powers that be didn't feel the need to go the extra mile. Therefore, it has to be manually switched."

Don stops him there and asked, "When it the last time they tested this generator?"

"It was tested a month ago and is good working order."

Mark continued, "Once the power does return to the gym, the diameter of the goals will default to the original eighteen inches. So, I will have to reprogram the app quickly to get back to our desired diameters on each goal."

"How long does that take?"

"About five minutes at most. I also have to plug in the code and the password which I have set up and have readily available. I have also installed on the walls behind the goals underneath the stands, a Bluetooth repeater/responder to give us increased range to successfully get back up to speed. You or I will have to physically go to reset these Responders, once the power comes back on. They're small blue boxes that are approximately five feet off the floor and the reset button will be right on the front.

"So, that is probably the worst thing that could derail us for the moment. Remember, it will take about forty-five seconds to get the goals to move back to where we want them."

"Okay, what's next?"

"Well, Dad, if some reason someone hangs on the goal and the referees believe the whole goal is comprised, then I'll have to get the ladder and they'll do the entire inspection again, height of goal and goal diameter. I'll have about one minute to reset the goal to its original diameter. That's very doable, since it'll take a couple of minutes to get the ladder out. I feel very comfortable in fixing this if such event occurs. We both know about this giant they have on their team and he could easily do this. However, I am sure a technical will be called on him, if he hangs on the rim too long!"

"Ok, what else?"

"That's all I could come up with, unless you see other difficulties we could face."

"Well, at least you've come up with two possible scenarios. I'll continue to drill down on it and you do the same."

Mark said, "Coach Al gave my contact number to the head Referee, Mr. J. Cain. Mr. Cain called me and wants to meet me an hour before the game to certify the new goals, height, etc. All gyms with new goals must go through this."

"I think that is smart and good," Don said. "It keeps us out of trouble once they've certified the goals."

They walked back into the house together and catch up on some sports while Lemmy, came in with his customary burst of energy, fired up about the coming game. He enthusiastically detailed Coach Al's game plan for Northern Penn. He told Don and Mark that *King Kong* cannot shoot free throws and that Empire must not let him get to the rim where he can dunk. "Foul him and make him shoot free throws! We'll double team him, once he gets to the top of the key and then try to stay on his four teammates by hustling our butts off. We will also do a lot of zone defense. Our offensive will run and move the ball quickly around the goal. I think we can win!"

Mark and Don liked what they were hearing but in an honest game, Empire, being an underdog by 15 points, really would have no chance. Mark winked at Don and the message was all about, "NOTHING BUT NET!" Don told Lemmy that he was excited about Saturday's game and that he was looking forward to it. They all then settled into a good meal.

Chapter 33

Friday morning, Don surprised Karen by telling her he was going to take the day off and take her for a ride in the country and get lunch somewhere along the way. She was so thrilled that they would get to spend time together. Don just needed to exhale from all the pressure he was feeling and to anticipate an end to the nightmare that was consuming him.

They headed west on State Road 51. It was a beautiful drive going through rolling hills and tree-covered vistas. They drove past a small strip shopping center about five miles from Empire. He noticed it was populated with the usual array of boutique shops, offices, and, he noticed, a quaint pizza parlor.

On their return trip home, he turned right onto a small road. The road was lined on both sides by trees and within about a quarter of a mile, the trees on the left opened up to a beautiful view of a large lake.

He stopped the car and they both got out to take a closer look at the lake. The road was some a hundred feet above the lake, making the view all the more spectacular. There was a real estate sign that proclaimed lots that were for sale and the name on the sign that read, "contact Bob Bunyan." Karen was quiet for several minutes before finally saying, "Don this is beautiful."

"How would you like to live out here?" he asked.

"What?"

"Well, Karen the boys will be gone in a couple of years and you and I can build a nice lake house with a deck and a party barge and just feel like we are on vacation every day."

Before Karen could respond, he added, "if you notice the lots face west over the hills on the other side of the lake and sunsets will be an everyday experience."

"Don, can this really happen?" she asked quietly, almost reverently.

"Of course. You in?"

Karen threw herself into his arms. "Yes, I am!"

"Great. let's get the ball rolling!"

They hopped back in the car but only after Karen had taken a dozen or so pictures.

As they head back town, Don again surprised her by stopping to eat at the pizza restaurant he'd spotted earlier. It had an authentic interior that created a feel of actually being in Italy. Candles on the table, white and red checkerboard table covers, soft Italian music and a wonderful pizza aroma. Don ordered a bottle of red wine and they settled in for what should be a home-spun pizza.

Their conversation was all about the future living in the lake house that Don would build. Karen said that she would begin looking at magazines with interiors that complimented the feel of lake living. Don revealed to her that he had already contacted the realtor and he'd be sending the subdivision restrictions to him. The lots were one-acre each and there were only four of them, meaning there would be few neighbors and he felt that was a good thing.

The pizza was delicious and the bottle of wine went down easily. As they headed back home, Karen held Don's hand just like the old days when they were dating: laughing and enjoying each other's company. Once home, she asked if he would like anything else to drink?

"I'm okay. However, I would like for you to join me for a nap!"

"I thought you would never ask," she said, smiling coyly.

It had been a perfect day for them as they reconnected and drifted off into a lazy afternoon. Before Don dozed off, he looked up at the ceiling and silently thanked God for a beautiful wife and a beautiful family. He felt so relaxed it was exactly what he needed before the stress-filled ballgame the following night. He was soon asleep.

"SATURDAY, GAME DAY"

Don arose at 7:00 a.m. sharp and was ready to enjoy a round of golf where he could try to keep his mind off of the game and his life altering bet. He arrived at the course around 8:00 a.m. and began to warm up. He soon learned that Vinney was on his team and they would be riding together.

Also on his team were two good friends, Bernie Nelson, who carried a twelve handicap and R.C. Ellis, the "A" Player, who was a ten handicap. Vinney was a fourteen handicap and Don was the anchor with a sixteen. Each team has an A, B, C, and D-Player and ranks were determined by individual handicaps. Everyone played off the low handicapper in the four groups this morning. His name was Tom-Tom Harris and he was a four handicap and was the reigning club champion. Accordingly, Don would get twelve strokes on the lowest selected holes as determined by the hole's handicap.

They were the first team to tee off on the number-one tee at 8:45 a.m. It was really cool how the score cards were computed. The starter on the first hole had a computer that had a program that printed the team's scorecard. Each member on the team gave the starter his member number and the program created to compute the card automatically filled in the card with the appropriate handicap holes for each player. It took about two minutes and *voila!* The card was handed to the team captain and off they went.

The winning team was determined by the best net score of each hole of the four players. Usually, a score of three- or four-over par for eighteen holes, would win. The entry fee for each player was thirty dollars and with sixteen players, the total prize money was four hundred eighty dollars. The winning team would split $280, second place split $120, and third place team split $80, and last place, zip. Of course, there were the usual side bets and that was lots of fun because a side bet could consist of a team bet, doubles bet or an individual bet. One could make a little extra money if he played well. Don had enjoyed a few good Saturdays – enough to buy steaks for the night's dinner.

He found Vinney to be in a talkative mood and he immediately began grilling Don on Empire's chances against Northern Penn. Don, a little put off by the probing and tried to end the talk by telling Vinney that according to Lemmy, Coach Al had come with a defensive scheme to limit Northern Penn's big Center. Also, Empire planned to press a lot on the inbounds pass in an attempt to reduce the thirty-second clock on Northern Penn's possessions. Don told Vinney in a slightly agitated tone, "Vinney, I have bet on the game. I believe in my son and we are the home team. I like my bet and I'm going to live or die with the results. Now, that's my take and you have to determine, if you are going to bet the game and which way to go."

"Well, Don, you have to look at the odds going up to fifteen-and-a-half points from twelve-and-a-half. Somebody, somewhere, really likes Northern Penn!"

"Damn it, Vinney, bet anyway you want. I just want to think about by golf game this morning, so let's do that, please.'

Vinney took the hint, if that's what one would call it and didn't talk about the game anymore. They both had fun and a good round. They finished around 12:45 p.m., grabbed a beer and a sandwich. Don told Vinney that he was headed home to get ready for the 6:00 p.m. game and if they won any money, he'd get it Monday at Vinney's Sports Bar. Their team shot a six over round and that usually doesn't pay anything, but who knows? Golf is a fickle game.

Don called Karen from the car and tells her he would be home shortly to take a shower and rest up for the game. He then called Deano's and made dinner reservations for 8:00 p.m. for six, anticipating that his parents would join them. Once home, Don learned that his parents were officiating at a wedding and they will not be attending the game or the dinner. He realized that he could drink freely during dinner, regardless of the outcome of the game. He said a silent prayer, asking God to forgive him for cheating and to please let the dinner be a celebration.

At home, he hopped in the shower and lay down to get mentally ready for what was promising to be a stressful night. He realized he was taking deep breaths to relieve his stress. *So much riding on this game, how in the hell did I get to this point in my life?* He tried to convince himself that Empire would cover the point spread and that the team would keep it close. *And oh yes, we have the goals on our side tonight! Thank you, Mark. NOTHING BUT NET!*

Chapter 34

Don was awakened by Karen at 4:15. He pulled her down to him for a comforting hug. *If she only knew what could happen if we lose this bet, she would kill me! Or even divorce me!* He got up and headed to the bath room to wash his face. He looked at himself in the mirror and was disappointed in himself as reality set in. He wasn't in control of the outcome. *I've done everything I could possibly do to win this bet.* He dressed and they walked out the door as he remembered the potential nightmare that lay ahead and it scared him to death.

As he and Karen were driving to the gym, she told him that there was bad weather on the way and would arrive around 7:00 p.m. Strong thunderstorms and wind were expected and that was why she'd brought an umbrella. Don's mind was racing and on so many other things that her words didn't register. They arrived at the gym at 5:00 p.m., parked and entered the arena. He heard the band warming up and could feel the energy starting to build as game time was only about forty-five minutes away. He spotted Mark headed to the store room to put the ladder up. Don told Karen to take her seat where they normally sit, perpendicular to the south goal and about ten rows up. He headed down and met Mark as he returned from the store room.

"Everything Good?"

"Yes, sir, goals are all certified by the head referee and we're ready to roll."

Don, unthinking, asked, "Have you fixed the goals?"

"Not yet, Dad, the teams are going to be warming up on them and I don't to tip our hand."

He realized how stupid his question was and admitted to Mark that he was a nervous wreck.

Laughing, Mark says, "Dad, we've got this!"

They were the exact words Don needed to hear at that moment. *My God, it's going to be hard to watch this game, much less breathe!*

Together, they headed up to join Karen and watch the warmups.

Suddenly, Don, stopped Mark. "Where is Mr. Lemoine? He had remembered Karen saying something about a bad storm that was heading their way. "Mark, if the power goes out, we need to get that generator up and going ASAP!"

"Yes sir. Mr. Lemoine and I are to meet in the bleachers behind Empire's Bench. He has the key for the switch over and we're ready for any eventuality. I even have an umbrella in case it rains and the roof leaks."

"Good man," Don said, relieved.

The game clock was set at thirty minutes and began its countdown to tip-off. The public address system crackles on and the announcer's voice boomed out over the spacious gym: "Welcome, ladies and gentleman, to tonight's game between the Northern Penn Golden Knights and the Empire State Blue Jays." As Northern Penn runs on the floor, he says, "Here are the Golden Knights! Polite applause ripples through the gym. Don's thoughts *were what a good-looking bunch of athletes*. Suddenly, the biggest human being he'd ever seen ran out onto the court. There he was, all seven feet, two inches tall and 320 pounds of him: "King Kong!" He was a giant as he towered over the rest of the team. The Knights are wearing a shiny golden outfit with black letters and black stripes. The uniforms screamed success as the team began to warm up on the south goal.

Then the announcer says, a little more enthusiastically, "And here are the Blue Jays as the band cranked up an energetic tune. "We look good too, don't we?" Don asked Mark, as much to assuage his own doubts as anything else.

Laughing at his dad's nervousness, Mark said, "This is going to be fun!"

Don remained captivated King Kong. His agility and his foot work belied his size. He was smooth and quick, unusual traits in such a large athlete. He had long black hair, a mustache, and a goatee. His wore a shiny gold shiny ring in his left earlobe. He wore a size seventeen shoe and his uniform was certainly custom-made.

He was a daunting presence and definitely not someone an opposing player would relish going up against. The publicity that preceded him was not hype; he was the real thing and there was no doubt that he would be moving on to the NBA, where he would be just another rookie until he proved himself at that level.

As Don watched, King Kong threw down a dunk so hard that when the ball hit the floor, it bounced all the way back up the bottom of the rim. The sound of the ball hitting the floor echoed all over the gym, like a rifle shot. If it was intended to intimidate the Blue Jays, it didn't seem to work. The team ignored the visitors as they went about their own warmup. Don, though, buried his face in his both hands, unable to convince himself that Empire had a chance – even with the goals rigged.

The horn sounded and the teams retreated to their respective benches. The announcer introduced each member of the starting team and when the Blue Jays' starters were announced, the home crowd cheered. When Lemmy was introduced, Don and Karen stood and clapped and yelled. Mark, meanwhile, had left his seat and was busily programming the goals before the tip-off.

Don's attention was focused on Mark, who gave the thumbs-up sign to his dad, indicating that everything was good. He then ran up the steps to rejoin his parents.

"We good?" Don asked under his breath.

"NOTHING BUT NET!" said Mark.

Chapter 35

Everyone stood for the National Anthem and then the announcer said, "Let's play ball!"

Both teams entered the court and the Blue Jays' big Ben prepared to face off against King Kong! Standing side by side, it was like David vs Goliath, just as Sally had described it. Ben was a good five inches shorter than Kong. There was no way he could handle this giant.

The Golden Knights would use the south goal in the first half and Empire would use the north Goal. They would switch for the second half. Mark, as planned, had set the south goal at fifteen inches in diameter and the north Goal at twenty-one inches, a decided advantage for Empire. The Referee blew the whistle and both centers prepared for the tip-off. The basketball was tossed thrown high in the air between both players and Kong slapped the ball so hard it hit one of Empire's player in the head and knocks him down. The ball bounced out of bounds. Because it was last touched by Empire, it was Golden Knights' ball. The game was underway in a most inauspicious manner.

The Knights inbounded the ball and headed for the south goal. Kong was already down at the south goal and was standing at the top of the key. Two Blue Jays were already standing in the lane, guarding his anticipated movement to the goal. Sure enough, he got the ball and immediately crashed toward the goal, knocking both Blue Jay players down in the process and getting charged with an offensive foul. One thing was evident early on: an opponent had to be brave to get in his way. He was like a bull running downhill.

Lemmy was all alone at the north goal and received a pass from Jessie, the Blue Jay forward. An easy layup and the Blue Jays led, 2-0. As the Knights inbounded the ball, Kong was on the wing, while the other players were on both sides of the Lane. One of their guards got the ball and passed it to Kong and this time he had a clear path to a dunk along the baseline. He didn't have to jump much as he slammed the ball into the goal and to his astonishment, the ball hit the other side of the rim and bounced out and is rebounded by the Blue Jays. Mark grabbed Don's arm and squeezed it. Northern Penn's shots will have to fit perfectly in the smaller rim! Blue Jays' ball and this time, the other Forward for the Blue Jays, James, hits a three-pointer from the top of the key. Five-zip, Jays! Don jumped up from his seat and was yelling loudly, "Go "Blue Jays, Go!" The home team fans start yelling, "Defense, defense!"

The Knights were not having success scoring and at the twelve-minute mark of the first half, it was Blue Jays leading, 11-4. Lemmy was on fire, shooting three-for-three from the floor. The Knights coach called a timeout. In the Blue Jays' huddle, Coach Al told the team that they needed to get Kong in foul trouble. He instructed Big Ben to take the ball in the lane and try his hook shot and maybe Kong would foul him.

Sure enough, the next time the Blue Jays were on offense, the ball was passed to Big Ben in the lane and he tried a right-hand hook shot from about four feet from the goal. The whistle blew, foul on Kong. He had literally knocked Big Ben to the ground and the home team fans were screaming for a technical. No such luck, however, but the Referee did go over to the huge center and gave him a stern warning. Don could swear he saw smoke coming out of Kong's ears.

At the five-minute mark of the first half, the Blue Jays held a 24-12 lead. The twelve-point lead, plus Don's twelve-and-one-half points, mean he was winning the bet by twenty-four-and-one-half points. Don had to stand. He felt like beating his chest to release his pent-up stress.

The Knights inbound the ball and as they were approaching their goal, there was a white flash of light outside that was easily visible through transom windows. The crowd reacted in a surprised collective murmur. The storm is definitely coming.

A Knight player was fouled and got two free throws. He missed the first and the second one barely fell in, making the score 24-13, Blue Jays. Coach Al slowed down his offense by taking the full 30 seconds to shoot the ball. Another streak of lightning lit up the night sky, but no thunder yet. Don thought the storm was at least ten miles away and should arrive by halftime.

Kong was now standing in the south goal's Lane and swatting balls down like the real King Kong did on top of the Empire State Building in the movie, only instead of the Empire State Building, it was Empire University. The irony was not lost on Don. The first half ended with Empire on top 26-15.

As the teams left the court for halftime, the band was playing the theme from *Rocky* and everyone was on their feet, clapping.

Don noticed that Mark had positioned himself under the south goal and is returning both rims to their original dimension for the second half warmups. More lightning strikes and Don took a look at his golf weather radar to determine where the storm's front was located. He figured it should arrive in about thirty minutes or less, which meant the second half would be underway by then.

He walked down the steps to meet Mark who was sitting on the bleachers near the south goal. "Mark, be ready. The worst should hit us in the second half, about five minutes in."

"Got it Dad. I'm preparing to reboot my app on my phone in order to reset the rims when the power comes back on. As you know, the rims will default to their original eighteen-inch diameters when the power is back.

Don, sounding more nervous than ever, said, "Mark, we can't fail, we have to have this game in our hands!"

"I know Dad, I know."

Just then, the teams come back on the court ready to do battle and Kong didn't look happy. He began practicing free throws, which he wasn't very good at and by throwing down hard dunks, which he *was* good at! The band was cranked up again and the atmosphere was electric, much like the atmosphere outside.

The Blue Jays got the first possession. Mark climbed the stairs again to be with his parents. He winked at Don and said again, "Nothing but Net!"

Empire's Forward, Jessie, hit a three-pointer from the wing, making it 32-15, Blue Jays. Don is starting to feel victory now as the Knights missed a three-pointer. Their shooting cannot find the bottom of the net and in most cases, the ball just bangs off the rim.

Deafening thunder could be heard as the lightning intensified.

The clock showed fourteen minutes and twenty seconds left in the game when a thunderbolt rocked the gym and the lights went out.

"Holy Shit," Don muttered to himself. In about five seconds, the emergency backup lights came on. The lights were scattered around the Gym and offered only limited light. There were many dark spots in the Gym but at least the emergency lights are concentrated around the stairs and exits. As the crowd groans at the inconvenience, a deafening rain began pounding the metal roof of the gym, sounding a hundred cattle stomping on the roof. More lightning and thunder and more intense rain as the storm grew louder by the second.

Chapter 36

Don was unable see across the gym to know if Mark and Mr. Lemoine had gone out to start the generator, though he was sure they were out there. Outside, Mark was holding the umbrella over Mr. Lemoine but it was to no avail. The wind ripped through the umbrella and both men were getting soaked. They hurriedly opened the gate to the generator and found the switch box. Mr. Lemoine opened the box and inserted the key and turned it to allow the natural gas to flow and the electricity to be shut off. More lightning and heavy rain and maybe the game wouldn't be completed. Those thoughts were not helping Don to resolve his life-threatening situation!

Of course, it took five to ten minutes for the generator to crank up enough power to bring the gym up to full power. The gym lights were the old mercury vapor kind that had to heat up slowly to provide sufficient light. There was an automatic sensor that allowed the electricity to flow through the bulb at the right temperature so as to not blow out the bulb. All one could do now was just wait for the system to get back up to speed.

Don saw when Mark and Mr. Lemoine reentered the small lobby from the horrible weather. Mark jumped into the training room located next to the lobby and shed his wet clothes, dried off, and found an old workout Jersey and sweat pants to wear. He also found dry socks and headed into the Gym and climbed up the steps to meet Don. He had a towel wrapped around his head and shoulders.

“Got it done,” he said cryptically. It’ll take a few minutes. I’ll have to go back down to the goals and be ready before the game continues.”

Don asked if Mark needed any help.

“No sir, we planned for this!”

In a few anxious minutes, the Gym lights flickered as the bulbs began to heat up. The game clock and scoreboard also saw some flickering and yes, it showed fourteen minutes and twenty seconds left in the game. Score: Blue Jays-32, Golden Knights-15.

After another ten minutes, the gym was restored to full speed. All lights were working, storm had moved on. The teams came back on the court and begin warming up again. Mark was down on the bleachers next to the south goal and he appeared to be working feverishly. The announcer said, “Play Ball!” It was the Knights’ ball and they immediately took it to the rim and laid it in for two points. The Blue Jays had the ball stolen from the inbounds and a two-pointer is made by the Knights Guard. 32-17, Blue Jays!

Empire didn’t look like the same team, missing from every angle. The Knights, on the other hand, found their footing and soon closed the gap to 35-28. Coach Al called time out. Don scampered down the stairs to where Mark was.

“What is going on?”

“Dad, I can’t get the app to reboot. Something is not clicking!”

Don was panicky! “Mark, think, what are we missing?”

“The Bluetooth’s not responding!”

Don remembers the boosters, Mark installed underneath the Bleachers on both the South and North Goals. “Mark, what about the Bluetooth Boosters?”

"Yes, that's it, go reset them, Dad, quickly!"

Karen noticed Don is running to the sides of the south goal bleachers and then disappearing underneath them. She thought maybe the electrical for the goals somehow got disconnected during the storm.

Don clumsily climbed over and through the support system for the bleachers until he spotted the booster. Meanwhile, the game was progressing at a fast pace and he could hear the silence on the Blue Jay fans. He reset the button on the booster and it turns green! He climbed back out as fast as he could and it was like Ali and George Foreman had each hit him on the chin full force. The score was Golden Knights 43, Blue Jays 38 with six minutes left!! Don knew that the Blue Jays could not compete with the Knights if the baskets were not rigged!

He walks up to Mark hurriedly and asks, "We good?"

"Not yet. Dad, go down to the north goal and reset that one."

Bam! The Knights hit a three-pointer! Lemmy hit a two-point jump shot, 46-40, Knights. Three minutes, ten seconds. Don, with the twelve-and-a-half points is winning, 52½ -46. Bam! Damn! Another three-pointer by the Knights. 49-40! Time out, Coach Al. *Thank God.*

The Blue Jays inbounded the ball and seemed not to be in a hurry. The clock needed to be on Don's side now. *Just do not let the Knights score anymore!* Big Ben was at the top of the key and attempted a three-pointer. It didn't even hit the rim, rebounded by the Knights. Kong, throws a long pass all the way across the Gym and goes over everybody's head, out of bounds Blue Jays ball. Less than a minute now. Don was praying for at least two points from the Blue Jays. That should cover the bet! Again, Don scrambled under the North Bleachers and reset the Booster, not that it would do it any good. Big Ben was fouled and missed two free throws. *This is a nightmare!* Less than thirty seconds, 50-40 Knights, no goal adjustments by Mark. The Knights' forward launches a three and is fouled. The three-pointer goes in and the Knights forward got a free throw to boot. He makes the free throw! 54-40 Knights!

Time out, Coach Al. Twelve Seconds left. Coach Al, emptied the bench except for Lemmy. Don was back up in the stands next to Karen. He desperately needed two points to cover! Mark was holding his hands up, like *I cannot believe this!* The Blue jays inbound the ball to Lemmy who raced straight down court and went in for a layup and was knocked to the floor. The Blue Jays bench emptied onto the floor and a fight almost erupts. Kong was not on the floor, otherwise no one would have dared go up against him.

His teammates helped Lemmy to his feet. It appeared that he may have been hurt. He was given two free throws – two free throws that he had to make if his dad was to win his bet. Don had both elbows on his knees and his hands were covering his face. He could not bear to watch. Karen leaned over and put her arm around Don and asked what was wrong. His whole future rested on his son's ability to make both free throws. If he failed, then it's "handcuff city!" If he succeeded, then Don would win his bet by the thinnest of margins, half-a-point.

"I'm just pulling hard for our son. Don peeked and saw Lemmy bouncing the ball at the foul line, getting ready to shoot the first free throw. Still unable watch, he would rely on the crowd's reaction to know if he made the first one. *Oh, if only that goal was at twenty-one inches in diameter, I would feel so much better. But it's only eighteen inches.*

Chapter 37

THE FREE THROWS

Karen still had her arm around Don's back. Suddenly, she jumped up and yelled. The first one was good and the fans acknowledged Lemmy's effort to fight through the pain. Don prayed, *One more Lemmy, please pull your dad out of the devil's pit.* He took a deep breath, still with his hands over his face, but with fingers spread in order to watch the second free throw.

Lemmy bounced the ball several times, looked up at the goal and then stopped bouncing and held the ball for what seemed to be an eternity to Don. He lifted the ball, bent his knees, and let it go! It looked a little long as it hit the connector, bounced straight up and finally fell directly into the net! The fans cheered. Knights 54, Blue Jays 42! Just four seconds left and the new players for the Knights raced down court and one launched the ball from half-court! The red lights glowed on the backboard as the ball headed for the goal, another heart-stopping moment for Don. The ball fell short of the goal, game over! Final Knights 54, Blue Jays 42 for the casual fan, but 54½-54, Don's favor!

Don began to bawl uncontrollably like a baby. He was unable to hold back the overwhelming emotion he had been holding on to for several days. Karen handed him a tissue to wipe his eyes. *I won, I won, I won, both of my sons pulled me out of my mess.* Karen sensed something deeper than a couple of free throws but did not ask the question of why he was so emotionally drained.

Don excused himself and headed to the men's restroom to dry his eyes and splash water on his reddened face. He was met by Mark who hugged him and walked with him to the restroom. After washing and drying his face, Don stepped outside to get some fresh air and to call Sally. "Please tell me you won!" she said when she answered, not bothering to even say hello.

Don, breaking down again said, "Praise God, I won the bet by half-a-point!'

"Go get a drink, we'll talk Monday and congratulations!"

Don walked back into the gym and greeted Lemmy as he exited the dressing room. Don, Karen and Mark gave him a hug as Don said, "Let's go eat a steak."

Don asked Karen to drive to Deano's Restaurant. Deano, a short Italian with a friendly smile, greeted them at the entrance and sat them in a circular booth in the rear of the restaurant normally reserved for VIPs. Merelene, their waitress, welcomed them and took their orders. Don, not wasting a moment, ordered a dry martini, chilled with one olive. Karen ordered a glass of Merlot. They were soon joined by the boys, who entered laughing and joking. Mark ordered a draft beer and Lemmy a large lemonade. Don felt like a million dollars and was determined to party like never before.

Once all the drinks were delivered, Don offered a toast to a great family and a wonderful game by Lemmy. He also congratulated Mark on ensuring the goals were certified by the head referee. Don, suddenly turning serious, looked directly at Karen and thanked her for being a great wife and great mother.

It took Don only two gulps to down his martini and he ordered another one as they ordered their steaks. Don was not stopping at two drinks. In fact, it was one of those times in his life that he planned on getting wasted! The pressure had been lifted and he felt like a million dollars with the knowledge that there would be no handcuffs in his future.

When the dinner ended, he held onto Karen as they walked out of the Restaurant, so other diners would not notice his drunkenness. Karen drove him home and he fell into bed and slept like a bear in hibernation. The boys headed to the college hang out, *The Blue Jay*. Don would be out for a long time as he slept off his wonderful day and celebration.

Around 7:00 on Sunday morning, he was awakened by his bladder, the most effective alarm clock there is. He stumbled to the bathroom and then it was back to bed. His head was banging away, but not enough to prevent him from soon falling back asleep. Around 11:00,, Karen woke him to let him know that she had let his parents know that they wouldn't be attending church this morning because their son wasn't feeling well. His mother told Karen that she would have them over sometime in the coming week and cook for them.

Chapter 38

MONDAY, A DAY OF REFLECTION

Don was still feeling a little weak when he arrived at the office around 10:00 a.m. on Monday. As he settled into his office chair, Matte brought him his coffee and he asked her to get Sally on the phone and please close my door. “She’s on line one” Matte said moments later. Don picks up, laughing.

“Well, aren’t you a “chicken full of corn!”

“You have no idea; you have no idea.”

“Well, you are as free as a bird, I got Golden’s report and you are clean, clean, clean!”

“Sally, there is a God above and I am so thankful that you had my back.”

“Don, nothing of this was your fault, we all just fell into a snake pit! As they say, you deal with snakes, you are bound to be bitten.”

“Well, Sally, life is an enigma; you think you are in control, but there are days where you take a wrong turn and the shit hits the fan!”

“I know, Don, but look, congratulations, I have to run, still got more snakes out there to kill, I’ll stay in touch, enjoy your freedom!”

“Good bye, Sally, thank you so much.”

Don took off to Vinney’s and found Mark already there, seated at the same high-top table.

“Dad, you look awful.”

“Yes, too much celebration!” Mark, before we get visitors here, I want you to promise me that you will remove your mechanical apparatus from the goals at the gym. Mark, this is very serious, very serious.

“Should any player hang on the rim and bring the goals down and they splatter all over the floor and it’s discovered the goals have been compromised, guess who they will point a finger at? Don Williams Construction Company, better yet, Don Williams.

“I will be ruined and I mean ruined! Do you hear me son?”

“Yes sir, Dad, I’ll put the goals back as delivered, I promise!”

“Son, please don’t ruin our family’s reputation.”

“I promise, Dad, I promise,”

At that moment, Vinney walked up, laughing and saying “You are one lucky Dog.”

“It’s better to be lucky than good!” Don replied.

“Well, I didn’t have to sweat as much as you, Big Dog!”

Don dismissed the veiled inference, saying, “How about those Blue Jays?”

“Yes, how about those Blue Jays? We got out of there just in time, especially you Don. Your son saved your ass!”

“Both my sons did a great job Saturday night!”

Suddenly turning prophet, he added, “In all my years, I have learned these things:

“Number one, Family is all about being a good provider, a loving husband and a loving father.

“Number two, A successful business is all about doing a good job at a reasonable price.

“Number three, Baseball is all about the Strike Zone.

“Number four, Football is all about controlling the Line of Scrimmage.

“Number five, Basketball is all about NOTHING BUT NET!

EPILOGUE

The Government charged the Lombart Savings and Loan and the Money Never Sleeps Development Company with Tax Evasion and named Dee Lombart, Fred Chicky and William Smith as co-conspirators in the indictment. They all pled guilty and were sentenced to three years in a federal prison camp and ordered to pay a fine of eight million dollars.

Sally O'Brian was initially charged with being a co-conspirator but cooperated with the government in untangling the values of the developments. For her cooperation, she was sentenced to one year of home confinement and no fine.! She had to surrender her attorney's license.

Golden and eight other Bookies were charged as co-conspirators and were sentenced to two years' probation and had to surrender their gaming licenses.

Two of the general contractors working for MNS Development were charged as co-conspirators and were sentenced to one-year home confinement and they lost their contractors' licenses.

Don Williams was never mentioned in the indictments. He and Sally moved to their new Lake House and enjoyed sunsets and fishing. The renovation of the Empire State University gymnasium was completed on time and under budget.

Lemmy graduated from Empire State with a sports management degree and with help from Sally's connections and her knowing the marketing head of the NBA's Philadelphia 76ers, Maryll Sanders, Lemmy was hired as an assistant.

Mark, after graduating, enrolled in Erie State University to complete his masters in mechanical engineering and got a job teaching freshman mechanical engineering at the college. He is also assisting as a consultant on the construction of the new Empire State basketball gym. Because of his experience with the renovation of the Empire State gym, he was asked to write the specs on the new basketball goals, similar to the ones that were installed at Empire State. Once the new gym was completed, Mark was confident that home games at the new gym would be successful and PROFITABLE.!!!!

NOTE TO READER: DON'T TRY THIS AT HOME

www.ingramcontent.com/pod-product-compliance
Lightning Source LLC
LaVergne TN
LVHW050556160826
845677LV00011B/2331

* 9 7 9 8 8 9 1 2 1 8 3 5 2 *